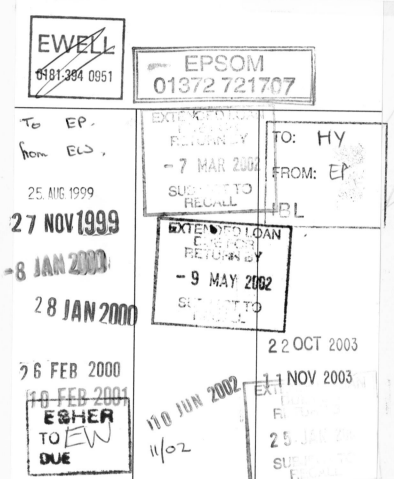

PATRICK NUTTGENS

UNDERSTANDING MODERN ARCHITECTURE

CAPTIONS BY

BRIDGET NUTTGENS

UNWIN

HYMAN

LONDON SYDNEY WELLINGTON

First published in Great Britain by Unwin Hyman,
an imprint of Unwin Hyman Limited, 1988

UNWIN HYMAN LIMITED
15/17 Broadwick Street, London W1V 1FP

Allen & Unwin Australia Pty Ltd
8 Napier Street, North Sydney, NSW 2060, Australia

Allen & Unwin New Zealand Ltd with the Port Nicholson Press
60 Cambridge Terrace, Wellington, New Zealand

British Library Cataloguing in Publication Data

Nuttgens, Patrick
    Understanding modern architecture.
1. Architecture, Modern—20th century
I. Title
724.9'1   NA680
ISBN 0-04-500040-9

Designed by Penny Mills
Typeset in Monophoto Photina by
MS Filmsetting Limited, Frome, Somerset
Printed in Great Britain at
The University Press, Cambridge

CONTENTS

The publishers and author acknowledge with thanks permission to use the illustrations on the following pages:

Abbott Hall Art Gallery 9; Wayne Andrews 46, 47, 202; Architectural Assoc. 96; Artek 137; Alvar Aalto 142; Architectural Review 177; Architects Journal 186; Arup Associates 198; Architectural Press 10, 15, 18, 19, 20, 21, 39, 46, 52, 59, 69, 71, 74, 98, 103, 107, 114, 115, 128, 130, 142, 149, 151, 153, 154, 155, 164, 173, 179, 189, 193, 194, 198, 204; British Architectural Library 7, 8, 16, 38, 42, 45, 69, 76, 82, 85, 86, 88, 91, 92, 111, 113, 115, 118, 119, 126, 147, 148, 160, 165, 166, 195; Graham Bowles 177; Building Design Partnership 178; Burrell Collection, Glasgow 184; Brecht-Einzig Ltd 206; Martin Charles 12, 168; CRM Society 51; Country Life 79, 81, 84, 86; Central Press Photos 182; Cement & Concrete Assoc. Library 200; Peter Davey 7; John Donat 163, 198; James Dunnett 203; E.T. Archive 125; Esto 200, 202; Frank Lloyd Wright Memorial Foundation 62, 66, 70, 71; Foster Assoc. 162, 166, 167; Fox Photos 181; Glasgow School of Art 55, 57, 58, 59; Glasgow University 60; P. E. Guerrero 74; Lucien Hervé 17, 98, 102; Hunterian Art Gallery 50; Hedrich-Blessing 62, 116, 127; Halifax Building Soc. 162; Hursley Lark Hursley 191; Lance Knobel 15, 17, 94, 101, 105, 117; Kimbell Art Museum 203; London Zoo 118, 191; Denys Lasdun & Partners 159; Roger Last 174, 175, 176; John Laing plc 198; MAS 27, 28, 30, 34; Museum of Modern Art 116; Museum of Finnish Architecture 132, 135, 139, 141, 143, 144, 145; Philip Molten 161; David Moore 196; National Trust for Scotland 52, 53; Richard J. Neutra 124; National Theatre 158; Royal Festival Hall 120; Steve Rosenthal 182; John Shannon 44; Ezra Stoller 75, 144, 200; St John's University Collegeville, Minn. USA 125; Swedish Museum of Architecture 135; Henk Shoek 175; Harry Seidler 196; Margaret Tomlinson 41; Times Newspapers Ltd 87; Thomas Photos 183; Jorn Utson 204; Morley von Sternberg 14; David Whiteley 122; F. R. Yerbury 96.

INTRODUCTION

The End of the Modern Movement

Sometime in the late 1960s or the early '70s, any consensus there may have been about the nature and purpose of modern architecture fell apart. Several factors were at work. Nearly 30 years after the Second World War, following one of the greatest building booms in history, the public could experience not just plans or ideas but the results on the ground. They didn't like what they saw. Nor did the vocal members of the great and growing Conservation Movement. They were convinced that anything modern would be worse than what was already there. Even more drastic was the demolition of major housing projects dating from both pre-war and post-war years, some of them famous examples of pioneering modern architecture. More serious still, never unanimously but very noisily, designers lost confidence in the Modern Movement.

It was all the more tragic in that that loss of faith represented the collapse of a major social experiment; for the Modern Movement in architecture was one of the great historical exercises in social idealism. Despite all the evidence of architectural history, it tried to prove that a valid architecture, with all the architectonic qualities that a great architecture ought to show, could be created for the working man, for the under-privileged no less than the privileged, for the mass and not just the individual, and at low cost rather than the handsome budgets of great historical works. Looking at it now with the eye of the immediate present it seems that it failed.

It is, in fact, deeply ironic that the two building types that are widely thought of as disfiguring the new urban environment should be mass housing and city development. Together they represent the area in which modern architecture should have been supreme, with its fundamental belief that architecture should be a positive protagonist of social reform in an egalitarian society. The problem with which we are now faced is to review this condition and see if there are any directions that would indicate a new central ideology, or whether we should simply accept that we are agents in a pluralist society with disparate and often conflicting values.

In recent architectural writing in the United Kingdom, two figures remain especially significant. One is Nikolaus Pevsner, whose *Pioneers of the Modern Movement* established for many people (including me as a student) the central meaning of the Modern Movement and identified the mainstream of modern architectural development beside which most other manifestations were aberrations to be condemned or, as in the case of Lutyens, ignored. The other figure is Sir John Summerson, whose RIBA lecture in 1957, *The Case for a Theory of Modern Architecture*, found the programme as the source of unity and the one new principle involved in modern architecture. The lecture had the same effect (upon me as upon others) as a seemingly inescapable truth about the Modern Movement. For anyone trying to design, as opposed to merely making comments – and that included teachers of design as well as practising architects – the case seemed to be made.

But there were always irritating difficulties. One of the recurrent problems about that theory of modern was the constant failure of the technology (or possibly of the architects' understanding of the technology) said to be the reason for the emergence of a new style – the plain rendered surfaces, the elimination of detail, the flat roofs, the mechanical services – that would make traditional features obsolete. There was always some uncertainty as to whether such failures were the result of ineptitude or of a vision that could not yet be realized in practice, an idea that preceded the technology reputed to have been the cause of its appearance.

The effects of technology can be negative as often as positive. Of no incident was this more demonstrably true than the event which effectually shook up all assumptions about the state of building. That was the energy crisis of 1973. It was an international crisis. Within a few years it was being recognized that, except in rare cases of phenomenal wealth, a suitable modern architecture of the approved kind could not rely on cheap energy for a totally controlled environment but would have to use traditional features, like opening windows and even pitched roofs. Architecture must once again become pragmatic, finding the simplest solutions to well known problems.

And that meant another change of heart and even a total change of direction. In contrast to the architecture that had represented the mainstream of the Modern Movement, it would now be concerned with the individual rather than the mass, with the personal rather than the anonymous, with the unexpected rather than the sustained programme of repetitive building types. The question now raised was whether a total architecture could again be generated, not by tackling the total situation but by the solution of individual, tangible problems. A theory that would justify such an approach must, of its nature, be different from the consensus which had been assumed in the teaching of many of us in the years following the Second World War. With a wealth of technological facilities available, it would lead, not as the pioneers had thought, to similar results, but to many different answers and even many different approaches – it would lead to an architecture of pluralism.

At this point it is best to explain something of the approach in this book, which does not follow the conventional path in aesthetics. Studies in aesthetics or the philosophy of Art are usually attempts to explain art in terms of non-art, to deal with the multifold problems of definition and reduce them to non-artistic terminology. However, architecture is never simple, has no one purpose and no one client. Of all the creative areas of human activity, architecture is the most multi-purpose, all-embracing, indeterminate and multi-level. And of no period in the history of architecture is that more true than of today, when many of the limiting factors of structure and materials have been pushed aside by technological development and replaced by new areas for exploitation and expression.

It therefore seems to me that the only credible approach to a theory of architecture for our own time is to follow the opposite direction. That is, not to eliminate the apparently superficial in an attempt to discover the meaning at the heart of things, but the very opposite – to widen the field of experience at the very start of the exploration so as to take in many of the new perceptions made possible by our highly organized world. It is necessary to accept as germane to any understanding of architectural development not only the conventional aspects of design like space, surface, mass, colour, detail, ornament as well as function, but to add to our perceptions the knowledge and experience of the natural and man-made worlds. In short, any positive new understanding of architecture must allow for a vastly extended understanding of function, of structure, of growth and form, of the psychology of behaviour and the mechanics of control. In such an understanding, the work of the architect is not to limit but to enlarge our experience, to be a medium for the enhancement of life rather than its reduction, for the revelation of possibilities in all their variety.

Whatever the field of examination, there is one dimension to architecture that marks it out as wider in its appreciation (or detestation) than any other art. That is its public dimension. Architecture involves the third person as a constituent agent in the creative process; it requires not only the creator and the client but the user and the observer; their tastes and wishes are part of the material out of which a new object is fashioned. The isolated artist has no role to play. Appearance may be sufficient for judgement in other arts but it will not be enough for architecture. Its uses are a constituent part of the totality that demands appreciation.

The uses commonly change; what is significant to the observer is the direct appreciation that the building is capable of being used. And that concerns more than the immediate client or the immediate user. All architecture – and certainly all great architecture – changes even as it is being built, is rarely the product of only one mind, is rarely wholly consistent and is constantly subject to change either by its users or by time and decay.

Nor will it suffice to note the words of the architects whose work is threaded through these pages. There are few areas of activity in which the leading professionals talk and write more incomprehensible and private jargon, thus distancing themselves from the users of their buildings and increasing the alienation of the architectural profession from the public. Such theorizing is important for the practitioners, enabling them to clear their own minds (if not those of anyone else) and canalize their energies so as to produce a recognizable and memorable object. A large literature exists of such thoughts and I have read most of it. The fact that it does not feature significantly in these pages reflects the conclusions I have reached through studying, teaching and constantly exploring ideas – that the truth for the observer is not in the verbiage but in the actuality.

It follows that if we are to look for an approach to architecture that is as wide as possible and encompassing the widest possible range of human experience, we will find the start of a theory not in philosophical speculation but in the ideas inherent in the buildings themselves. This is especially so of those which we recognize as having responded to the demands of their users (or potential users) as well as to the technology of their time. In them we might discern the springs of an intellectual structure which would be relevant in further creative development.

But which buildings? To answer the question we need to go back to roughly the turn of the century, when, I believe, many of the themes of our time were taking shape and when a sophisticated consciousness laid the foundations for a rich architectural experience. It might have been one of the great movements of history – and perhaps it was since its development was continuous and all that was lacking was its recognition. It has, sadly, disappeared behind the wordy clouds of the International Style developing in the 1930s. However, if we start an investigation the other way round from the usual – being inclusive rather than exclusive – we might find the International Style to be the interruption not the climax, the aberration not the mainstream. And where would we look for the mainstream? To the period when the new architecture was taking shape – that is, to the 50 or so years around the turn of the century.

This was possibly the last time when there was a coherent movement – not of sameness or repetition, but of an astonishing variety and a great richness of personal experiment and expression. Nor was it a phenomenon peculiar to Britain. It was a good period for most of Europe and certainly for the United States. What they all had in common was, paradoxically, their individuality, their search for a national, idiosyncratic architecture, along with their exploitation and refinement of building construction and services. It was the period when building construction was at its best, achieving standards never reached before or, in ordinary day-to-day building, since. So, the argument of this book starts at the turn of the century and specifically in the 1890s.

CHAPTER ONE

THE TURN OF THE CENTURY

The period between roughly 1890 and the outbreak of the First World War in 1914 represented a major stage in the evolution of architectural design. At the time it looked as if it was the start of a rich and fertile movement – not a standard international style but a family of styles and building types, more varied, original, colourful and idiosyncratic than ever before. What interrupted that tradition was first the War, which occupied many of the creative energies of the countries affected and witnessed the destruction of much creative talent. Then, in the '20s and '30s, in all countries, the financial slump, unemployment and other social and economic disasters dried up the supply of architectural commissions.

The years with which this chapter is concerned must have been years of prolific optimism. They are crucial to any understanding of the foundations of 20th-century architecture, if only because of the dramatic contrast between the condition of the majority of the working population and that of the more leisured classes in which the arts flourished. At that time, the problem for the theorist of art and architecture was to work out how the discoveries made in the established arts could be applied to and developed within the lives of the less privileged – a social problem reflected in all the arts.

Nowhere more than in architecture. Economic, political and social changes are factors to which architecture cannot help responding. They affect taste and style and scale; more fundamentally they affect the types of building that can be erected and the budgets within which they have to be built. And also their style. At the turn of the century the search by architects in many countries for a free style – one untrammelled by history, especially the history of elegant buildings, of palaces and monuments – was in effect the search for an architecture that could be relevant to all people and many diverse situations.

Changes in society would themselves have made such a search desirable. The Great War, the Russian Revolution that accompanied it and the end of several empires that followed it, made the War a turning point. Reading the literature and viewing the arts of

House at Bedford Park, London, sometimes called The Grey House: Charles Voysey (1891)

Voysey had been working in architecture (and designing wallpapers and furnishing fabrics) for 14 years before he built his first house in 1888, thus making his active architectural life contemporary with the younger Lloyd Wright in America. Voysey was a tough little man and he built tough, homely, lovable houses. This London house for J. W. Foster came three years later. From the outside it shows little of his interest in Tudor and Stuart architecture for it is a tall box, three floors high, covered in grey rendering. Its shallow, hipped roof and asymmetrical projecting square bay on the first floor make it appear very modern, something of a holiday villa, very continental.

(Above)

The Red House, Bexley Heath, Kent: Philip Webb (1859)

Built for William Morris when Webb was 28, the Red House is an early and definitive example of the 'honest' architecture they pioneered. The construction is substantial and homely in appearance: it is both domestic and vernacular – even has a whiff of the oasthouse about it. Detail is sparse, but red brick and tile exhibit their own beauties frankly. The plan is free and innovative, producing a massing of units on the exterior and a roof silhouette strongly evocative of the mediaeval. Oddly, like many Victorian houses, it faces north, an orientation that was discarded in the next 50 years by its followers in domestic Art Nouveau.

the preceding years, it is difficult to escape the impression of a society hectic with energy as if it almost had a sensation of the disaster that was about to befall it. If so, that consciousness must have been heightened by the knowledge of discoveries being made in science and technology and the arts.

The last decade of the 19th and the first decade of the 20th centuries witnessed important discoveries in radioactivity and the development of radio signals, in diesel engines and aeroplanes, in X-rays, in the definition of plutonium and radium and electrons. It saw the publication of the theory of relativity, the development of quantum theory and discoveries of viruses and the manufacture of vitamins and aspirins.

In literature it was the time of Oscar Wilde, H. G. Wells and George Bernard Shaw; of Housman, Conrad, Hardy, Kipling and Conan Doyle; of W. B. Yeats and J. M. Synge; of Mark Twain and Henry James; of Nietzche, Zola, Chekhov and Kafka. In the visual arts it was the time of Cezanne, van Gogh, Gauguin and the early Picasso; of Beardsley, Klimt and Munch. In music it saw the first performance of pieces by Bruckner and Mahler, Richard Strauss and Debussy; by Elgar and Stravinsky, Puccini and Scott Joplin. In structural engineering it saw the Eiffel Tower and the first Chicago skyscrapers.

The architecture that characterizes the period is one of the most rich and diverse in architectural history, reflecting a mood that could alternate between adventure and romance and tragedy,

Broadleys, Lake Windermere: Charles Voysey (1898–9)

Broadleys is usually considered Voysey's most original and finest work. Like Baillie Scott's Blackwell House, also built in this fashionable area of Lake Windermere, it was not a 'country house' in the sense of belonging to a landed family and being situated on their estate. Rather, the new breed of country houses were summer holiday houses built for rich industrialists. Broadleys was built for A. Currer Briggs, a coal magnate from Leeds. It stands on a terrace above the lake and is emphatically horizontal with sweeping roofs and bands of windows which ripple into three bays on the lakeside. The central of the three bays lights the hall which is boldly carried up into the second storey. Affinities can be seen with the contemporary Chicago houses of Frank Lloyd Wright in the free planning of space. It is now a boat club.

between personal exploration, new perceptions of man and nature and new discoveries in science and technology. Like the other arts, architecture reflects a mood in which artists are reacting as much against the trends of the time as in accordance with them. The major figures – Gaudi, Lutyens, Mackintosh and Lloyd Wright – whose work will be considered in detail in later chapters – all started their architectural practices in the 1890s. For the moment, though, we must look at the architectural context in which they were able to flourish – in three main areas; Britain, Europe and America.

The British Isles produced one of the most distinctively national architectural movements ever to come from those countries; yet one whose character was to spread rapidly to the Continent and influence the design not only of buildings but of all sorts of artefacts big and small. That was the Arts and Craft Movement. Its prophet was the prolific designer and writer, William Morris. 'Have nothing in your houses,' he wrote, 'that you do not know to be useful and believe to be beautiful.'

Visually, its products were influenced by the Pre-Raphaelite School, to which Morris belonged. The Pre-Raphaelites believed that since it was Raphael who had directed painting into a formalism that was now dead, the work of the painters who preceded him would reveal a truth to nature and an honesty missing from contemporary work. It is no great distance from that belief to Morris's identification of the useful and the beautiful and in particular to seeing the crafts – the design and making of things for ordinary day-to-day use – as the basis of an artistic movement. And if it could contain everything within the house – the tapestries and furniture, textiles, tiles and glass, knives and forks –

Blackwell House near Bowness, Westmorland: Mackay Hugh Baillie Scott (1898–9)

Blackwell House was the summer house of Sir Edward Holt, brewer, paper manufacturer and twice Mayor of Manchester. It is Baillie Scott's largest house and belongs to his young, free and Art Nouveau period before 1906. He published his work (realized or projected) in *Houses and Gardens* in that year, and with Voysey had considerable influence both in Britain and on the Continent. Muthesius speaks of him as 'the first to have realized the interior as an autonomous work of art. ... Each room is an individual creation, the elements of which spring from an overall idea.' He also rejoiced in bright colour such as citrus lime, lemon and orange, red and sharp blue.

Externally, the simple Scottish lines and white harling betray Scott's descent from minor Scottish aristocracy and perhaps anticipate Mackintosh, as do some of the interior fittings, notably the slim, white-painted wood planes of the drawing-room mantelshelf. But the plan is free in the Voysey/Frank Lloyd Wright manner, with low public rooms grouped on either side of that distinctive English Art Nouveau feature: a two storey, multi-purpose living hall. This is overlooked by the gallery which gives access to bedrooms. Here, the hall is almost over-the-top Arts and Crafts, resembling an Elizabethan inn courtyard, roofed over; it is half-timbered and sports a minstrels' gallery with a deep inglenook below.

as well as the house itself, there opened up the potential of a great movement capable of creating the unity of all things, a wonderful conspectus in which everything could be good and honest and well made.

And more. It was central to the Arts and Crafts beliefs that art is for everyman – what Morris called 'the well making of what needs making'. The Arts and Crafts could therefore be an important, if not central, element in the movement for social reform.

If the artist was himself responsible for what he thought, made and sold, then he would be a key figure in remedying the general scene of personal irresponsibility. Art could stimulate social reform by being an answer to social problems. And where would you find the model for such an admirable society? You would find it in the Pre-Raphaelite *social* scene – in England in the mediaeval village. So C. R. Ashbee, having founded a Guild of Handicrafts for working men and women in the East End of London, moved his company to the Cotswolds, to Chipping Campden where it seemed the crafts could flourish. In fact, he moved away from the necessary markets and within a few years the Guild had to be wound up. But the idea did not die.

What made the movement known throughout Europe was the publication of *Das Englische Haus* in 1904 by Herman Muthesius. Muthesius had been an attaché at the German embassy in London and being an architect had used his time to carry out a thorough and detailed study of new houses; the four volumes were in effect a critical catalogue of the architecture of the Arts and Crafts Movement. It described and illustrated many of the houses – Morris's own Red House at Bexley Heath by Philip Webb, Voysey's houses like Perrycroft at Malvern of 1893 and Broadleys on Lake

Church at Brockhampton, near Ross-on-Wye, Herefordshire: W. R. Lethaby (1900–2)

This 'cathedral in miniature' is off the beaten track. The solid walls of red sandstone, short square tower at the crossing, thatched roof, clapboard and shingle cladding on the tower over the south door, and doves cooing in the belfry – all suggest a time-slip back to a more stable and naïvely worshipping age. Inside, the mediaeval atmosphere persists. The nave vault sweeps up from floor to roof ridge in one continuum. Light floods through Christopher Whall's stained glass, spilling jewels of colour across the floor. There are tapestries by Burne Jones and the stalls are expertly carved. But an abrupt transition from past to future occurs in the roof, where pre-cast, unreinforced concrete is sandwiched between the external thatch and the pointed ribs of the vault. This device for coping with problems of condensation, insulation and the maintenance of an even temperature, has made periodic reappearances since in the work of modern architects, using grass as the insulator.

Windermere, Baillie Scott's Blackwell House of 1890. Perhaps the most paradigmatic building of the movement was W. R. Lethaby's church at Brockhampton near Ross-on-Wye with its concrete roof structure covered with thatch.

The architects of the Arts and Crafts Movement never solved the problem of creating artefacts and buildings cheap enough for the common man. Instead, as William Morris himself admitted, they catered for the better off – the prosperous middle classes who could afford to live the simple life. And that was true for the contemporary work on the Continent.

There the style of the architecture was more conspicuously that of l'Art Nouveau, popularized in illustrations and posters by Aubrey Beardsley in Britain. Again, as in Britain, the source of design was nature, especially the darker and danker corners of nature like ponds and creepers and tendrils and roots and leaves. The signature of many works was the whiplash line and the rejection of the rectilinear. The new forms suggested mystery and movement; they used new materials or treated old materials in a new way; they were used for all objects big and small, especially the small – details, junctions, precious artefacts. Beardsley's influence is clearly to be seen.

The most complete expression of the movement in Europe was the work of Victor Horta in Belgium. He achieved, it was said, the three-dimensional equivalent of the two-dimensional inventiveness of the book illustrators. Like the exponents in Britain, Horta also saw his work as part of the movement for social reform and one of his major works was the headquarters of the socialist party in Belgium, the Maison du Peuple of 1896–8.

The application of a new style to new kinds of building was wholly appropriate in any country. Like Horta in Belgium, Hector Guimard in France created a style – in this case for the Paris Metro. In Austria, J. M. Olbrich attempted to create a new style in the Art Gallery in Vienna's Friedrichstrasse. Henry van der Velde, working in Belgium and Germany in every medium, was another socialist concerned with every detail and every artefact. Some of the most imaginative buildings were those by Joseph Hoffman in Brussels and Hendrick Berlage whose Stock Exchange in Amsterdam was a stunning demonstration of the kind of space that could be created by the new structural understanding of traditional materials. The most extreme statement of uncompromising rejection of traditional decoration was that by Adolf Loos whose statement that 'Ornament is a Crime' was not altogether confirmed by his own work.

It was in America, as well as in France, that the next major element in the discoveries of the turn of the century were to affect the future of architectural design.

Although concrete had been used by the Romans and later

Tassel House, off Avenue Louise, Brussels: Victor Horta (1892–3)

Viollet-le-Duc's design for ironwork supports, English chintzes and wallpapers such as those used in the Tassel House dining-room, local Rococo stucco work: all have been put forward as influences on Victor Horta; but the final verdict always appears to be that Art Nouveau in Belgium sprung, full-grown, from the head of Horta in the shape of the Tassel House. The restrained exterior does nothing to prepare one for the lyrical and linear fantasy within. Horta broke with the traditional Belgian plan of repetitive floors, the rooms opening off corridors; and substituted a new way of breaking up the total space, using a staircase sweeping up from a free hall to give access at different levels.

Tassel House-Interior

This hall is the most photographed part of the house and has been variously described as a 'veritable manifesto of Art Nouveau' and 'hysterical linearism'. Wall coverings, mosaic flooring, cast iron banisters and light fittings flow and flick freely all over the place, never repeating themselves as counterpart English designs do. They incorporate Horta's famous 'whiplash' line and much that looks like musical staves and clefs gone vegetative. But the motif is not limited to decoration: the cast iron pillars of the structure also shoot and uncurl long leaves to carry the staircase. His ironwork is probably his greatest achievement. Horta made a speciality of rich men's fantasies, contrasting rich materials, and opening fairytale vistas through dining-rooms to winter gardens or up through swaying stairwells. But he also built the Maison du Peuple, for the Brussels branch of the Socialist Party.

Entrances to Metro Stations, Paris: Hector Guimard (1899–1900)

The influence of the Ecole des Beaux Arts where Guimard studied, the Arts and Crafts movements of England and Scotland which he visited in the 1890s, and, of course, Horta, are all apparent in Guimard's work. He is the first and greatest of the French Art Nouveau designers, giving a very personal expression to abstract biological and botanical motifs in a wide repertoire of materials – brick surfaces and furniture, for instance, as well as superlative ironwork. These are clearly seen on the gateways to the metro stations, and in other works such as the Maison Coilliot, a little ceramic shop in Lille, where there is scarcely a straight line even in the structure: the upper floors are hollowed out, the halls, stairs and doorways hooped and coiled and writhing.

(Opposite, above)

Wiener Sezession Exhibition Hall, Friedrichstrasse, Vienna: Joseph Maria Olbrich (1899)

The exhibition space was built for the Vienna Secession – the society of artists founded in 1897 in revolt against the establishment Academy who limited exhibits strictly to 'fine art'. In contrast, the Secession

Gallery exhibited across the board, even building replicas of C. R. Mackintosh's rooms for one exhibition. The Wiener Secession can therefore be seen as the start in a progression via the artists' colony at Darmstadt (to which both Olbrich and Behrens were to belong), to the Bauhaus. Olbrich's insistence on expressive geometry for the Gallery designs also moves in this direction. Neo-classical and Art Nouveau influences are, however, still apparent in this work: the massing is reminiscent of Schinkel; and the extraordinary central dome composed of metal fretwork in the shapes of leaves and florets (so that it looks as if a clipped mulberry tree had thrust its way through the roof) certainly owes much to Horta and Guimard.

Palais Stoclet, Brussels: Josef Hoffman (1905)

Built outside Brussels for a Belgian financier, Adolphe Stoclet and his wife Suzanne, this house is a scene for gracious living in the contemporary idiom. Here, Stoclet's art treasures were to be displayed, and an elegant and artistic life carried on. Hoffman, a disciple of Otto Wagner, responded to the brief with a sophisticated Cubist exercise in planes, emphasized by contrasting dark borders. He uses rich, smooth marble and expensive woods, and an expansive plan where clever changes of axes extend the spacious atmosphere. On the exterior, bay windows mark the position of the main rooms, such as the hall and music room, and the staircase is enclosed in a stepped tower (somewhat incongruously decorated with figurative statues) that rises above the roof surfaces. The narrow stair window running the height of the house was to prove a seminal feature.

Berlage inspired the Amsterdam School of Architects and it was his writings that made Frank Lloyd Wright known in Europe. He was influenced by the growing labour movement and planned low-cost housing in Holland. His winning design for the Amsterdam Stock Exchange shows his devotion to undecorated brick walls (which he liked to use inside as well as out) combined with strong Roman arches. The walls of the main hall are cut away in tiers of broad arches reminiscent of the Colosseum, and it is roofed with an exposed steel structure.

builders, it did not become a widely used material until the introduction of steel rods to bond with the concrete made reinforced concrete the most flexible as well as powerful structure. That development happened mainly between 1870 and 1900 – with experiments in Germany, America, England and France. But it was the systematic exploitation by François Hennebique that transformed structural engineering. By the time of the Paris Exposition of 1900 his firm, protected by patents, had become international.

The architectural possibilities of this were dramatically demonstrated by Anatole de Baudot in the church of St Jean de Montmartre begun in 1894. His younger contemporary Auguste Perret is usually credited with creating a more consistent architectural statement, notably in his own apartment block at 25 bis Rue Franklin where the use of both a concrete frame and lifts made an unusually flexible open plan possible.

In Chicago, the changes were most spectacular. Why Chicago? By one of those chains of coincidence, everything seemed to come

Apartments at 25 bis Rue Franklin, Paris: Auguste Perret (1902–5)

The flats were built on a concrete frame of rectangular panels, similar to a wood frame construction. Projecting bands of windows, made as large as bye-laws would allow, gave views of the Seine and the Eiffel Tower. Perret found the concrete structure facilitated several features that Cobusier was later to publicize – the freeing up of the plan; allowing open areas interrupted only by supporting stanchions on the ground floor (into which Perret moved his office); provision for car-parking and a roof terrace on the top floor; and through space in the living rooms.

together in Chicago making possible a unique flowering of architecture at a moment of fundamental change.

The economy was booming; immigrants, flooding into America and setting out for the west, stopped in Chicago as they headed for the sun-drenched slopes of California. Chicago itself was a ramshackle, largely timber-built town, which had grown from 50 people in 1830 to 300,000 in 1870 and 500,000 in 1880. In 1871, its greatest disaster struck – the fire which spread across the river and destroyed more than half the buildings. It was a disaster for many citizens, but for the city itself and the professionals involved in building, it was the greatest opportunity they had ever had. Architects and developers flocked there. Within 20 years, Chicago was in the forefront of architectural endeavour. By the 1890s, it was witnessing the rapid fabrication and opening of some of the wonders of the New World. The skyscraper had been born.

It was not just a technological episode. Both before the fire and shortly afterwards, architecture had begun to reveal itself in a native, new tradition. In that, Henry Hobson Richardson was probably the most influential designer. Unlike most of his contemporaries he had travelled to Paris to study at the Ecole des

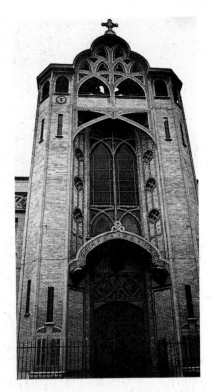

Church of St Jean de Montmartre, Paris: Anatole de Baudot (1894–1904)

In this church, de Baudot combined a metal roof structure with reinforced concrete. The church illustrates the two sides of de Baudot's architectural life: as a disciple of both Labrouste and Viollet-le-Duc he restored mediaeval buildings, but spent the latter years of his life in experiments with brick and concrete.

Beaux Arts. But he had found the style of teaching suffocating, with its insistence on the logical use of historical exemplars, and returned to America convinced that a valid architecture for his country must be found in the traditional architecture of its own history – the vernacular, not of the Indians but of the settlers and their successors. Richardson therefore found in their solid, stone, massive architecture his own native style. And that fundamentally influenced the emergent Chicago School.

If Richardson found in the solid traditional buildings of the mid-West the foundations for a new, untrammelled, free style independent of European motifs, there was another tradition of building in the mid-West which was of the utmost importance in the rapid colonization of the prairie lands and the erection of new clapboarded houses and barns that were the new and more basic vernacular. The use of the balloon frame, with its simple frame structure that could be knocked together with nails, was sufficiently stable without the elaborate jointing with dowels and mortices and dove-tailed joints of traditional high-class joinery. The builders now wanting to go high, who started to do so with massive masonry, had to make little imaginative leap to recognize

Marshall Field Wholesale Store, Chicago: Henry Hobson Richardson (1885–7)
This assertive block in red Missouri granite ashlar with brownstone above proved that commercial buildings could also be dignified and monumental. Richardson's Beaux Arts training shows in this palazzo for a new Renaissance. On the exterior the levels are defined by apparent arcades, created by grouping the ample fenestration so that it spreads horizontally across the walls. Both fenestration and load-bearing courses vary from bottom to top, so that the upper levels seem lighter as they approach the decorative cornice. Inside, its seven storeys is another matter: timber floors are supported on a skeletal construction of wrought iron beams and cast iron columns.

the fantastic possibilities if the buildings were to be framed rather than monolithic. All that was necessary was the materials. And if reinforced concrete was on its way, steel was produced in abundance. The invention of flanges and the perfection of the I-beam followed by welding joints instead of bolting them provided everything necessary for the great leap upwards.

Reliance Building, 32 North State Street, Chicago: Burnham and Root (1890–1904)

The 16-storey Monadnock Building, Chicago, a very urban and industrial block in solid masonry, was nearing completion when the same architects started on its much slimmer, more sophisticated metal-framed successor, the Reliance Building. Eventually reaching 13 storeys high, this is probably the most perfected expression of light-flooded, multi-storey architecture of the period. Both these sky-scrapers were made possible by Siemen's invention of the electric lift, and by Burnham and Root's own introduction of spread foundations to carry tall buildings on soft soil.

The first truly framed structure was the work of William le Baron Jenney who, like Richardson, had studied in Paris. He had studied engineering but became, in effect, not only an engineer but an architect and highly successful organizer of building projects. His Leiter Building of 1879 (demolished in 1972) is generally regarded as the first recognizable structure of the Chicago School.

Of the partnerships that effectively transformed the city of Chicago and then the urban structure of many other cities, the most definitive were those of Daniel H. Burnham and John Wellborn Root, whose Rookery of 1886 and the Monadnock Building of 1889–91 were immediately recognized as major developments. Burnham went on to become a city planner, producing the Chicago plan of 1909. Another celebrated partnership was that of William Holabird and Martin Roche which produced some 70 buildings in the central commercial area of Chicago, among them the Tacoma Building of 1889 and the Marquette Building of 1894.

Ultimately the most influential partnership was that of Adler and Sullivan. Louis Sullivan had studied briefly at the Ecole des

Auditorium Building, Chicago: Louis H. Sullivan (1886–9)

Sullivan's first great work (now Roosevelt College), the Auditorium is a massive block with a somewhat Italianate tower which sheltered the Adler and Sullivan office. Clearly influenced by Richardson's Field Store, Sullivan made a similar division of the façades, roughly into thirds horizontally, but here the arcade effect across the middle range is much more blatant with a row of giant orders holding up the round-headed lights. The construction is still solid masonry, so Sullivan used a heavy granite for the base and a light stone above. The complex incorporated an office building and hotel as well as a theatre, and afforded plenty of scope for rich and characteristic Sullivan ornament.

Beaux Arts in Paris and Dankmar Adler was an engineer, older than Sullivan. In Chicago they formed a partnership in 1881 which broke up in 1895; but by that time Sullivan had designed the Auditorium Building of 1886–9, a fantastically original structure bringing together an hotel, office and theatre for more than 4,000 people. On his own he produced his masterpiece, the Carson Pirie Scott store (originally the Schlesinger & Mayer store) of 1889–1906. And that, with its wide spans and dimensions dictated by functional needs, its repetitive exterior and original decorative entrance, brings together most of the strands of the new architecture.

Carson Pirie Scott Building, Chicago: Louis H. Sullivan (1899–1906)

This was Sullivan's swan song. Although built in three phases and eventually finished off by Burnham to Sullivan's designs, the verticality characteristic of his architecture was retained in the curved window bay on the corner that carries right up the height of the building from the rounded entry pavilion. 'Form follows function' said Sullivan, and his differentiation of the essential functional elements in this building made it the prototype for countless 20th-century offices and department stores. There are two floors of offices, covered in white terracotta tiles hung on a steel frame, and punctuated by even rows of large 'Chicago' windows. These floors sit on a two-storey base (which is what a shop needs) framed as part of the metal structure.

Sullivan was a passionate prophet of the new architecture, a gifted writer whose statements have ever since had the authority of classical simplicity. 'Form follows function and this is the law' became a central slogan for the Modern Movement. In *The Autobiography of an Idea*, he brought an impassioned prose to bear on the development of the idea: 'It is the very essence of every problem that it contains and suggests its own solution'. His phrase, the 'ten fingered grasp of reality', indicates the almost poetic fervour with which he announced the architecture of the new practical world, freed from historicism and the tyranny of the historical styles. Frank Lloyd Wright was in his office for several years and he described Sullivan as the 'Lieber Meister'.

At this turning point in the fortunes of architectural design it is useful to summarize the situation and indicate the forces that effectively changed the scene for ever. First, the turn of the century witnessed the climax of a tendency inherent in the work of the 19th century – the end of the authority of the styles. Whether they were Classical or Gothic with all their variations, the styles were worn out and the search was on for a genuine style of its time. That involved not only the rejection of stylistic forms but of the very method of design. The Beaux Arts tradition of continual refinement of a grand idea until it might achieve practical relevance was superseded by a more pragmatic process based on functional need and structural change.

For those who started with a traditional style, influenced by their education and training, the sequence of change was a familiar one in the history of architecture, moving from copy to analysis, to the extraction of principles of design rather than the imitation of architectural forms and thence to a genuine originality. In that, Gothic had more to offer than Classical. Practitioners and theorists had revealed the possibilities in extending Gothic through the new structure and the new materials.

But more fundamental was the recognition that a new, free architecture was necessary because of the emergence of new building types for which there was no provenance in the history of styles. The major new buildings – as the more observant must have noticed in the 19th century – were no longer churches, palaces and country houses. Nor, by the end of the century, railway stations and factories. They were a vast programme of building types – schools, colleges, park buildings, libraries and, above all, offices. They were buildings not for one client or one family or one firm. They were buildings that had to cope with lots of people. The social dimension was fundamental to the movement. And so must be the problem of cost.

Yet underlying all the vitality in all the continents was a theme that reflects the need to find something fundamental in architecture, something so real that from it a new style could be rationally

Ironwork Details, Carson Pirie Scott Building, Louis H. Sullivan (1899–1908)

The lower floors, and particularly round the entry, are covered in the most bizarre iron filagree ornament – an exercise in personal fancy markedly in contrast with the strict rationality of the main floors. Sullivan designed these himself, full-scale using his own technique for the production of twisted naturalistic forms.

developed. If the traditional styles were now seen to be superficial, where was the new source for invention and originality?

You might find it in the ordinary buildings of ordinary people, which must be more basic than exercises in pretension or self-conscious display. That meant the rediscovery of the vernacular, as we shall see in Chapter Three. But that in turn must lead back to something still more fundamental. The search for a free style, free from the shackles of history and scholarship, reflecting the new discoveries in structure and materials, must in the end return to something so real and so final that it can only be the ultimate authority for architectural form – Nature. Nature must offer, as it was increasingly investigated, the ultimate authority. It is a theme which recurs throughout the late 19th and the 20th centuries and it is not yet exhausted.

Its most brilliant and original expositor at the end of the 19th and the first 20 years of the 20th centuries was possibly the most original architect ever to practise in Europe. That was Antonio Gaudi and it is to his work that we must now turn.

CHAPTER TWO

NATURE, STRUCTURE AND GROWTH

The Imagination of Gaudi

The rise and fall and rise again of Gaudi's reputation is almost a barometer of changes not just in taste but in the understanding of the modern architectural movement. After a period of obscurity it now seems that he may represent some of the most fundamental and lasting forces in design. And that is a revolution; for whatever his reputation when he died, he was seen for over 30 years as simply an eccentric figure with a gift for extraordinary fantasy, unbalanced and possibly insane. Because his personality was so unusual and his position in the architectural scene unique it is necessary to explore his personal story in order to understand his designs. It is a story in which no incident was more vividly symbolic than his death.

On 7 June 1926, at about 6 o'clock in the evening, an elderly man crossing the road at a busy intersection in Barcelona was hit by a trolley-bus and knocked senseless to the ground. He was an unkempt figure, with white hair and a white beard. He looked like a tramp. Several taxi-drivers refused to take him to hospital. In the end someone was persuaded to carry him to a local clinic, from which he was moved to the paupers' Hospital of Santa Cruz in the old quarter of the city. He died there three days later.

By that time he had been found by friends and identified as Antonio Gaudi, probably the greatest architect ever produced by Barcelona, and certainly one of the greatest architects in the history of Spain. He was also, despite his personal obscurity and appearance, a celebrated Barcelona personality. For ten days the incident was continual news in the Barcelona papers; his death was described as a national calamity.

His funeral procession, from the hospital in which he had died to the Cathedral and then to the Church of the Sagrada Familia, of which he had been the architect, was a fantastic Spanish occasion. The procession following the hearse was nearly half a mile in length. A crowd of many thousands lined over two and a half miles of streets along the route. He was buried in the crypt of the unfinished Sagrada Familia by special dispensation of the Government and the Pope.

About the man and his work there is no shortage of written material. Over 20 films have been made about his work, together with more than 60 books and at least 2,000 newspaper articles. And yet, for all the literature, there is very little information about Gaudi as a person. For one thing, his studio in the Sagrada Familia and all his files were destroyed in July 1936 in the early days of the Civil War; he was only rediscovered in the 1950s and seen in the 1960s as a representative of Art Nouveau. For another, he was difficult to understand. He spoke in Catalan on principle.

Gaudi was born at Reus in the Campo de Tarragona in 1852 where his father was a coppersmith. He studied architecture, briefly and erratically, in the University of Barcelona. He was a liberal, an anti-clerical and a dandy. When he took over the design of the Sagrada Familia at the age of 31, Gaudi would visit the site in an open carriage and give his orders from the carriage. He was of medium height, with a blond beard, long hair and blazing blue eyes. He never married, nor did he ever leave Barcelona except for a short trip to the South of France, to Morocco and to Castile for the building of one of his designs, the Astorga Palace, in 1887.

Gaudi's first architectural works included street lamps and features for public parks. In 1878 he began work on a summer holiday house for a tile merchant, using the tile as a module for the whole house. He produced no drawings but sat under a parasol and personally directed the work. The popularity of the house led to other commissions, the most celebrated of which was the gate between two pavilions at the entrance to the Guell estate in Barcelona – a fantastic dragon made of materials ready to hand, semi-abstract, highly expressive. The dragon, the symbol of Barcelona, became a constant feature in Gaudi's work.

But if he could have been seen at first as mainly a decorative artist, his work rapidly indicated an exceptional understanding of structure. He found the parabolic arch a sound and economic structural form, and used it throughout his career. In the episcopal palace at Astorga, for instance, he introduced original structures like the fan-shaped triple arch of the portico. It was too complex for the builders though, and he eventually had to build it himself.

The integration of decorative and structural originality can be seen in the Casa Batllo on the Ramblas, the great pedestrian avenues in the middle of Barcelona. Gaudi recast an existing structure, giving it a winding staircase through the middle and a façade which caused the building to be known as the House of the Bones. The projecting members of the lower floors look like shin bones. In mathematical terms they are hyperbolic paraboloids.

Gaudi must have been one of the first major architects to use a structural form which (as we shall see later) has become well

Dragon Gate, Guell Estate, Barcelona: Antoni Gaudi

The pavilions at the entrance to the Guell estate on the north-west edge of the city (where the university is now) were built between 1884 and 1887. Gaudi also restored the old house. The gate became a well-known feature in Barcelona. Gaudi seems to have seen the dragon as a symbol of barbaric force, tamed by St George, the patron of the city. Note the apparently screaming mouth, the semi-abstract form, the use of materials found ready to hand – tiles, pieces of iron, disused objects – to create an animistic and evocative work of art.

Casa Vicens, Barcelona: Antoni Gaudi

The summer holiday house for Manuel Vicens was begun in 1878. Vicens manufactured a tile 6ins square and Gaudi used it as a decorative feature and module for the whole house. The brick walls are covered with ceramic. The railings are of wrought iron in shapes based upon natural tangling forms. Gaudi's first house is a Barcelona expression of Art Nouveau.

known in recent years through the work of Felix Candela and others. Gaudi explained his fascination with warped surfaces by references to his descent from a family of coppersmiths. 'All these generations of people concerned with space', he said, 'give a preparation. The smith is a man who can make a volume from a flat sheet. Before he begins his task, he must have visualized space.' The geometrical shapes which fascinated him were the paraboloid, the hyperboloid and the helicoid.

His main client was Count Eusebio Guell, a textile magnate of enormous wealth. For him Gaudi designed a palace in the middle of Barcelona, with parabolic entrance arches opening into the vestibule and a huge central saloon cutting through several floors and capped with a perforated dome. Still more original was the park he laid out for Guell on the north of Barcelona. A dragon covered in ceramics crouches at the entrance and steps lead to a market hall in the form of a Greek temple with an open air theatre on top and a serpentine bench around the edge covered with ceramics arranged by Gaudi himself. There are several miles of viaduct with drains through hollow columns leading to an enormous cistern which was to have supplied a whole village if that had ever been completed.

Incomplete as it is, the Parc Guell is a stunning display of artistic and structural ingenuity. It is loved by artists like Salvador Dali and by the children who play there today. Gaudi saw it as an opportunity for a poetic metamorphosis. The Doric columns of the market hall lean inwards; the shape of the galleries expresses the thrust and movement of structural forms. Looking at Nature for his justification, Gaudi pointed out that 'God's architecture has no straight lines.'

The control of space in three dimensions demonstrated by Gaudi in the park was further exploited in what must be the most singular block of housing ever designed. The Casa Mila – la Pedrera, the Quarry – provoked cartoons when the scafolding was removed and balconies looking like seaweed, ceilings looking like sand marked by waves and an entrance looking like a grotto were revealed. There is hardly a straight line in the place. But, above all, the roof is the most complete expression of structural ingenuity leading to an apparently crazy landscape.

The changing levels are, in fact, logical, being the result of the varying heights of parabolic arches in a top floor with varying floor spans. Gaudi had created an extraordinary flowing land-scape of changing levels and shapes.

The building, still unfinished, with which Gaudi will always be identified is the one on which he was working when he died. That is the Expiatory Temple of the Holy Family, the Sagrada Familia, the building which was to become his life's obsession. It was begun in a neo-Gothic style by a well-known Barcelona architect,

Teresian College, Barcelona: Antoni Gaudi (1888)

The exterior is characteristic of Gaudi, a relatively simple main block and wrought iron railings based upon natural forms. The interior is one of Gaudi's first uses of parabolic arches as structural forms, creating an interior much simpler and more austere than much of his work.

Francisco de Villar, in 1882. But de Villar resigned and in 1884 Gaudi took over and totally transformed the building.

The promoters intended to create a building which would use the image of the Holy Family as an exemplar of domestic life, with St Joseph as the patron of the working class. The building would itself be an expiation of sins in a materialistic age. Gradually abandoning all his other work, Gaudi devoted himself to the project, ultimately going to live on the site. As a preparation for designing the building, he buried himself in the study of the liturgical year.

Casa Batllo, Barcelona: Antoni Gaudi (1904–06)

Gaudi recast an existing building, gutting the inside and then recreating it with, through the middle, a winding stair whose twisting timber forms express movement and flow. Window details are based on natural forms. The furniture, including matching armchairs in the dining room, was also designed by Gaudi. The façade was totally redesigned with projecting windows on the lower floors which are hyperbolic paraboloids but look like shin bones. The house, on the Ramblas, the pedestrian avenue in the centre of Barcelona, is known as the House of the Bones. The roof is shaped like a huge sprawling dragon, with its backbone forming the ridge of the roof.

The liturgy became for him a source of beauty in religious ceremonies and a key to the meaning of life. And he increasingly saw the great temple as the vehicle for the Liturgy. That recognition coincided with a spiritual crisis. In Lent 1894, shortly after he had taken over the building, he carried out a fast so extreme that he was confined to bed until Palm Sunday and nearly died. He gave up his smart clothes; he took no more pay; he donated some of his properties to pious causes. He lived nearly all the time at the Sagrada Familia, taking only a rudimentary meal at noon prepared for him by the caretaker, and even giving some of that to a mouse that ran about the place. He gave up wearing

The Guell Palace, Conde del Asalto, Barcelona (1885–1889): Antoni Gaudi

Also built for Count Guell, this was both his town house and museum for displaying his antiques and a centre for concerts and exhibitions. It has parabolic arches opening into the vestibule so that guests could drive carriages inside and walk up the stairs to the *piano nobile*. The carriages were left at the back and the horses were led down a spiral ramp to stables in the cellar. The central room, or saloon, cuts through several floors of the building, a continuous space with a perforated dome that gives an impression of stars by day and light by night. The rooftop is characteristically fantastic.

underclothes and wore the same suit until one of his assistants insisted on his changing it.

Construction was at first slow and it was only with the design and completion of the Nativity façade that the idea began to take shape. A huge donation then enabled him to change the plans and complete four huge towers on that façade. Gaudi worked out the symbolism in detail. The apse with its pinnacles represented the patron saints and the Blessed Virgin Mary. Each transept was to have four towers and the three transepts would thus have twelve towers, representing the twelve Apostles. In each transept façade there would be three porches, representing Faith, Hope and

The Parc Guell, Barcelona: Antoni Gaudi

On the north side of Barcelona, the park was laid out between 1900 and 1914. Guell admired the English theory of the Garden City and hoped to create a garden village in what was then open land. There were to be 60 triangular sites but only three houses were built, one occupied by Gaudi until he moved into the Sagrada Familia. It was not a success as a village. The intended Plaza became a playground for children. Note the undulating wall which forms alcoves and playseats, and the coloured treasure-trove of the ceramic crazy paving. The present school was originally Guell's residence. Gaudi's house is now a museum.

Charity, with Charity in the centre. At the crossing inside there were to be four enormous structural columns, representing the four Evangelists, holding up the centre of the building.

Thus, the building was to be a poem in stone and he himself would lecture to visitors, allowing no interruptions, seeing architecture as a means to a more perfect society. The temple was not, as many people thought, a piece of fantasy. 'Fantasy,' he said, 'is born of a deformed reality and peopled by ghosts. Imagination is a

The Sagrada Familia, Barcelona: Antoni Gaudi

The Expiatory Temple of the Holy Family (Sagrada Familia) was originally designed (by de Villar) in neo-Gothic style. Gaudi took the work over in 1884 and transformed the design. The irregular income from donations made it inevitable that the work would proceed in phases and by the time of Gaudi's death all that had been completed was the apse walls and the façade of the south transept, the Nativity façade. Work is now continuing and if the temple is ever finished it will be one of the biggest cathedrals in the world, with a central tower higher than the 12 transept towers – more than 500 feet high. The three portals of the Nativity façade represent Faith, Hope and Charity. The Charity portal is in the middle.

product of a real image.' If it had any originality, that was because, in his most memorable dictum, 'originality means returning to the origin.'

In the twelve great towers were to be 84 tubular bells, sounded by electrically operated hammers or compressed air. They would have been enormous; the base 'F' bell was to be 20 metres long. The towers were conceived as sounding boards, and the louvres that punctuated their sides as the stair spirals up inside the tower, were openings through which sound would be able to reach the whole of Barcelona. The Nativity façade would have tubular bells; the Passion façade tubes like an organ; the West façade would have ordinary bells. He spoke about magnificent architectural concerts that would be held there and heard throughout the city. 'Architecture and music,' he said, 'are the arts of space and time respectively. It could be said that architecture is the music of space and music is the architecture of time.'

The towers would give out not only sound but light. Two-thirds up their height, their pinnacles would contain conical holes for spotlights to light the street and the great ciborium that was to rise over the crossing. The whole Temple would have been a colossal dragon, breathing fire but now the servant of God.

The almost obsessive iconography of the building as a sermon can be seen in the façade he himself completed, the Nativity façade. Gaudi had identified himself so wholly with the Temple and its symbolism that he had begun to carry out in stone abstract ideas and spiritual concepts that were essentially immaterial. There are rays cutting through the atmosphere, snowy icicles about to melt, incense surrounding the monogram of Jesus, night and light and clouds and space. He had tried to transcend the limitations of physical reality and created instead what he deplored – a fantasy.

By the end of his life he was the recluse in the temple, taking people round, speaking only Catalan, spreading his kindness and his vision to everybody. He refused to pose for photographs, which were only taken of him when he took part in processions. He walked around as a beggar, begging for alms for the building of the temple – a visionary, it was said, who walked the streets carrying the temple inside him.

If the Sagrada Familia is his most famous building, the chapel for the Colonia Guell, Santa Coloma da Cervello, is the most original. Gaudi was commissioned in 1898. He spent ten years making studies and began construction in 1908. Only the crypt was finished. But the unfinished church had led to Gaudi's development of a new method of working out a structure.

He saw the possibility of making a significant improvement upon Gothic. Gothic he disliked; he thought it incomplete and an architecture of formulas. Flying buttresses he described as crut-

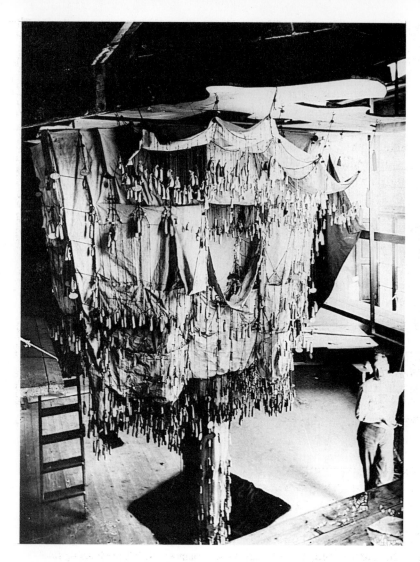

*S. Coloma da Cervello –
Funicular Model: Antoni
Gaudi*

Turned upside down, the photograph
indicates the shape of the proposed
church.

ches to prop up the building. 'The Gothic,' he said, 'is an art of formulas. My aim is to improve that style.'

He devised a 'funicular model' – essentially a diagram of stresses made in three dimensions with non-elastic cords, using the same number as the proposed number of arches and ribs. The hanging cords represented the arches and ribs which would form the roof structure. From the cords were hung weights corresponding to the loads on the arches and ribs. The hanging cords were thus distorted into a strange polygonal form. If this were then photographed and turned upside down it would give a logical design for a structure in which the tensile stresses exerted on the cords were now reversed and converted into compressive forces. That meant that an unusual and fluid shape could be made up from ordinary objects like stones, bricks and cement, held in compression. If, instead of the cords or inside them, sheets were used, he could arrive at the right warped surfaces, the correct shape for materials in compression.

As the structural design progressed, he became convinced of the mystical qualities, as well as mathematical fascination, of warped surfaces. His comments on the site were put together by his biographer, Martinell; 'If we imagine them to be infinite in extension, the generatrices of ruled warped surfaces constitute infinite space. Such surfaces are the paraboloid, the hyperboloid and the helicoid. All three have the same elementary structure which is represented by the tetrahedron. A tetrahedron with unlimited faces is the synthesis of infinite space. The first of these surfaces could symbolise the Trinity, while the second represents light, and the third movement. The paraboloid is generated by a straight line that slides along two others. If we imagine the three straight lines to be infinite, then the three form a totality which is one, indivisible and infinite – qualities which coincide with the essence of the Trinity. The hyperboloid, because of its regular and gradual form with the generatrices spreading out from the throat, represents the radiance of light. The helicoid because of its resemblance to the growth and development of certain plants, is movement incarnate.'

Whether or not Gaudi's ultimate identification of three-dimensional geometry with spiritual meaning is helpful to people who do not share his mystical vision and faith, there is no doubt of the importance of his discoveries in structure and form for the

Crypta Gaudi, Church of S. Coloma da Cervello: Antoni Gaudi

Gaudi was commissioned by Guell to design the workers' village for his factory. He left the housing to assistants but designed the church himself spending ten years (1898–1908) making studies and devising the structure. Only the crypt was built in his time and Gaudi personally supervized the work; the upper part of the church is by another firm. Despite its appearance, the crypt is built of stone. Grilles and window frames were made from scrap iron from Guell's works. There are virtually no vertical lines; the angles and slopes of the structure were derived from his use of a 'funicular model' described in the text. The columns left unused for the upper part of the church lie in the surrounding garden. The exterior colonnade is a stone structure formed from hyperbolic paraboloids.

future of architecture. He may have seemed eccentric; he cannot have been mad. His approach to structural design is rational and the survival of his buildings, however bizarre their form might at first appear, is evidence of the soundness of his structural understanding.

Furthermore, he was well read, familiar with books by the significant aestheticians of his time, devoted to Ruskin's works. And he was a celebrated figure in his native city. Barcelona was in the midst of a huge expansion caused by the development of commerce and industry. Like many other towns in France, Germany and Britain, it sprouted separatist groups interested in local culture, the vernacular, folklore, regional literature and art – a movement towards freedom and the inspiration of Nature in opposition to traditional forms.

Gaudi was designing at the climax of the period of Art Nouveau, known in Barcelona as *Modernismo*, and the signs of it are all in his work – the use of iron, of beaten metals, the hatred of straight lines, the use of the whiplash line in furniture and spaces, the determination to be a craftsman on the site rather than an architect in an office. In all of that he might have been typical. But he was undoubtedly more. He designed in the most individual style we have ever seen, and he opened up structural possibilities that he found in nature rather than in books.

How does one summarize the characteristics of such a very personal corpus of architecture? It is an architecture of sunlight, full of colour, based upon Greek and Arab decoration, a product of Spain, with details that seem half maritime and half continental. Its shapes reflect nature; they also reveal his interest in mechanics and in three-dimensional geometry, a growing obsession with ruled surfaces or warped shapes generated by straight lines, like hyperbolic paraboloids. Traditional details are changed. Columns incline and lean to express the direction of the forces which they are resisting. It is an architecture of prolific invention.

He discovered a great deal of his inspiration in nature – in the sea, in small things, in plants; but also in barbaric manifestations of nature, like the great rocks that soar up over the monastery of Montserrat, the great mountain with the volcanic teeth. He had worked with de Villar on the restoration of the monastery and was moved more by the natural formations that surround it than by the buildings themselves. He was fascinated by the shapes of mouths, of sea-ways, or rock formations, and he found original forms in the organic structure of trees and their branches. He was probably the most original and inventive architect of his time. And his discoveries have not yet been fully exploited.

CHAPTER THREE

THE VERNACULAR AS INSPIRATION

If Gaudi discovered a source for original and expressive structural design in Nature, he was equally insistent, to use again his most celebrated aphorism, that originality meant going back to the origin. For him, that was a religious rather than aesthetic conviction. What made him an original for us was his exceptional mind and imagination. In his attitude to historical styles and his search for a basis for design more fundamental than any of them he was not alone, either in Barcelona or in most of Europe.

He reflected in that statement a widely felt need which is probably always lurking in the back of the minds of architects but never more than at a time when the authority of the styles was under attack and some other authority had to be found. It meant a search for some more fundamental validity, a search vividly expressed in Louis Sullivan's phrase, 'a ten fingered grasp of reality.' That search for reality we shall see reiterating itself throughout the story in this book. At this stage, it had a special meaning. For if there was to be a new architecture, freed from the shackles of historic styles which were identified with privilege and prosperity, it must be an architecture relevant to everyman. And where would you look for an architecture that served everyone, however humble and unprivileged? You would find it in the ordinary houses of the ordinary man.

It is difficult to exaggerate the importance of this reorientation of architectural endeavour, this widening vision. For it strikes at the very heart of the conventional definitions of architecture. To take a contemporary definition, by Nikolaus Pevsner at the start of his *Outline of European Architecture* (1943), 'A bicycle shed is a building. Lincoln Cathedral is a piece of architecture. Nearly everything that encloses space on a scale sufficient for a human being to move in is a building; the term architecture applies only to buildings designed with a view to aesthetic appeal.'

The difficulty with that kind of definition – and the many others that have sought to distinguish architecture from mere building – is that it is more difficult to establish what is aesthetic appeal than it is to group together a lot of buildings and call them architecture. A

definition of aesthetic appeal is an exercise in philosophy and probably endless. How much simpler and more egalitarian to throw all the building types together and call them architecture; and then see if there is any agreement that some are better than others. What a relief from social blame and distinction if every building is architecture! And possibly the more ordinary the better.

In the attempt to create a new architecture relevant to its day this could imply at least one of two approaches. On the one hand it might be possible to create an architecture *without* style. That was a possibility but reached its apogee and its most uncompromising statement after the First World War; we shall see that in Chapter Eight. On the other hand, it might be possible to use one's knowledge of everyday architecture, the houses of the ordinary man, as a vocabulary in the design of a consciously inspired architecture, a new style valid for more people than before, less pretentious, more real. That was the emerging trend described in Chapter One. It is now worth studying the principles behind that and note the far reaching implications of the study and use of the vernacular.

The Orchard, Chorleywood Hertfordshire: Charles Voysey (1899–1900)

Voysey's own house at Chorleywood could be used as a catalogue of Art Nouveau details: white walls, black woodwork, bands of vertical windows. There is strong vertical emphasis indoors too (for instance in fireplace overmantels at picture-rail height) and heart-shaped cut-outs. In this house he made use of his gift for designing wallpaper and hangings in which he rivalled his teacher, Macmurdo.

72 and 73 Cheyne Walk, London: C. R. Ashbee (1897) (now destroyed)

Ashbee's building work is mostly either in Chelsea or around Chipping Campden in Gloucestershire, the Cotswold village to which he moved his Guild of Handicrafts from London in 1903. The Chipping Campden community of 1500, originally somewhat hostile at the influx of 150 London Bohemians and their families, gained architectural and social advantages from the Guild's presence – as well as a place in history. In the brief 12 years of the Guild's stay, Ashbee built houses and cottages in the area, a three-storey former silk-mill was renovated for workshop premises, valuable pieces of mediaeval architecture were conserved and social facilities for both adults and children were set up. These included a museum and a library, brass bands, cookery and joinery classes, drama, gardening, swimming and citizenship classes. And a laundry for starching local collars. 'In London, Ashbee was trying to create a new, picturesque, changeful Chelsea in place of Georgian regularity and uniformity', says Peter Davey. Sadly, only two of the group of houses in Cheyne Walk (38 and 39, built in 1899) now remain. Something of the freedom of patterning made possible by his superb sense of proportion can be seen in the fenestration and details of ironwork on nos. 72 and 73. Inside, there was equal attention to detail with fireplaces covered in brass, and much thought put into the evolution of suitable light fittings when electricity took over from gas.

The word 'vernacular' is mainly used about language. It comes from the Latin word *verna* which means a home-born slave and came to mean native or indigenous. More pertinent to this study it means 'not of learned formation'. In language it signifies the language or dialect of the country. In architecture it came into use about 1839 and was used to describe the minor buildings of town or countryside.

But by the end of the 19th century, the interest in the vernacular had become obvious in many other aspects of life as well as architecture. A considerable regional literature had become successful not only in England but in Scotland and France, Germany and America. The vernacular in the form of Folk Song had been collected by Cecil Sharp and Ralph Vaughan-Williams and then in a natural way begun to be incorporated into major music such as Vaughan-Williams' own symphonies. It was accompanied by a greatly increased interest in rural and urban crafts, in artefacts of every kind, in what came to be known as the History of Everyday Things. Taken to extremes it could, in due course, become a perversion like Hitler's obsession with the idea of the Herrenvolk.

What it must mean for architecture is that it includes the simplest of dwellings, built in the simplest way – and that means functional buildings, without pretension, which at their simplest are shaped by two factors – where you have to build and what you have to build with. The fascination with the vernacular therefore involved a new interest in regional and local architecture in contrast with the internationally known styles of Classical and Gothic design. As if echoing the regional literature of novels and the study of local customs and crafts, vernacular architecture depended upon the use of local materials and details of design that could cope with local climate. At first put up for immediate and thus usually temporary use, it had become more permanent during the periods of great rebuilding in England in the 16th, 17th and 18th centuries.

To quote Ronald Brunskill's authoritative study of *Traditional Buildings of Britain*: 'So the term "vernacular architecture" has been adopted to define that sort of building which is deliberately permanent rather than temporary, which is traditional rather than academic in its inspiration, which provides for the simple activities of ordinary people, their farms and their simple industrial enterprises, which is strongly related to place, especially through the use of local building materials, but which represents design and building with thought and feeling rather than in a base or strictly utilitarian manner.'

It was part of the consciousness of the turn of the century, and beyond, that the source of ideas was far from limited, that the vernacular contained an unexhausted wealth of ideas and details

The Barn, Foxhole Hill Road, Exmouth, Devon: Edward Prior (1896–7)

Edward Prior considered Nature to provide the 'ultimate facts behind all architecture which has given it form', particularly the irregularities of natural growth, 'the constant slight deviation from the ideal, in which is the genesis of beauty.' In a lecture in Edinburgh in 1889, he spoke of the materials he liked to use: 'velvet thatch, soft warm tile, silver splashed lead, hoary roughness of stone. ... These are Nature's own textures for us to use ... we may borrow from her and show the grain and figure of her works ... we may leave our wood and stone as it comes from the chisel or the saw.' Not surprisingly, Edwin Lutyens was to be influenced by the theories and experiments in free plans and massing of this man, who worked for a time with Lethaby in Norman Shaw's office. For The Barn in Exmouth he used a butterfly plan. On the ground floor the diamond between the top of the wings is filled in with a terrace to the garden; above, on either side of the central gable, tall round chimneys rise like antennae, and long eaves sweep down low over the wings on either side. The walls are of an organic mixture of dressed stone and rubble, so that it fits easily into the site. The original thatch was replaced by local tiles after a fire soon after it was built.

with an enormous variety caused by the local limitations that led
to one solution to a problem rather than another. Seen on a world
scale, the treasure of architectural ideas was inexhaustible. Seen
even in one country there was a wonderful variety of forms and
materials, of colour and texture. If the great historical styles had
been exhausted, or if a thinking architect wanted in any case to
escape from their tyranny, all he had to do was look out of the
window and go out to explore the material ready at hand. And
that was more than just another style; for the vernacular carried
within itself a special feature usually unremarked by the architectural theorists of the historical styles.

This was reflected in the work of the Arts and Crafts Movement
– the recognition that a valid style for the everyday starts not from
the design of the whole and then proceeds to the design of the
details but from a detail so well studied and tried that it is known to
work and can be used with confidence. And more than that – the
detail becomes the key to a style of architecture – an outfit of
working details become the vocabulary of the building.

That is to say, a well thought out and proved junction between,
say, two materials or between a wall and a roof or a corner, or the

solution of a valley in the roof and the ridge can, if extended throughout the whole buiding, become the basis of design. And that applies to all sorts of components – not only parts of building construction but artefacts and details, balusters, stair treads, door latches, handles, virtually everything. It carries a still further meaning. If the solution of a detailed problem can lead to a style it must be the way in which that detail is solved that suggests whether the architecture is good or bad, true or untrue, valid or unvalid. The test of a good design is whether it solves the problems 'with style' – or apparent ease or relaxed conviction. To illustrate this crucial part of modern architecture we need only to look at two countries where it had a lasting effect – that is England and America – where the vernacular became a true inspiration for major architecture.

In Britain, the most celebrated exponent of the vernacular was Charles Annesley Voysey (1857–1941). Voysey was not a craftsman himself but a gifted designer who understood materials and was able to communicate a happy atmosphere. He loved and knew plants and started as a designer of wallpapers and textiles. He only started designing houses in 1889, and by 1900 he was the most popular house designer in the country. His houses are suitably plain and informal and above all comfortable. Broadleys has a most simple geometry and simple components like unmoulded mullions and sloping buttresses on the outside nicely linking the house to the ground. The Orchard at Chorleywood could hardly be simpler, white walls and unpainted timber, with vertical stair balusters going up the whole height, wrought iron hinges to the doors – a delightful exercise in apparent simplicity that depends upon profound thought and strict selection.

M. H. Baillie-Scott (1865–1945) produced the archetypal English house which influenced suburbia as it spread along the main roads. If possible, his houses had a central hall with rooms opening off it and there were inglenooks, music galleries and wide stairs. About Edwin Lutyens (1869–1944) and Charles Rennie Mackintosh (1868–1928) there are special chapters in this book; both were masterly users of the vernacular in their domestic work. E. S. Prior (1852–1932) was a scholar of English mediaeval architecture who attempted to revive local styles through the use of local materials, like flint, tile and brick, sometimes mixing them all in a distinctive and thus somewhat unvernacular way. In Yorkshire, Walter Brierley brought all these themes together and created not only thoroughly English houses but also some of the most outstanding Board Schools following the Education Act of 1870 which made schooling available for all children.

But the outstanding personality was W. R. Lethaby (1857–1931), a major writer whose books had wide influence. As Principal of the Central School of Arts and Crafts between 1893

St Andrew's Church, Roker near Sunderland, Co. Durham: Edward Prior (1904–7)

The brief called for a church to seat 700 and to be a coastal landmark for shipping. Prior responded with a massive stone structure whose outline could be that of a goal or castle or fort. It has a square tower and a wide nave, its vault appropriately ribbed like the upturned hull of a vessel.

Scarcroft School, York: Walter Brierley

Walter Brierley is known as the Yorkshire Lutyens, just as Sir Robert Lorimer is known as the Scottish Lutyens. Brierley's houses are smaller scale than those of Lutyens and Lorimer, but share the same move to quality domestic architecture of a scale which is manageable without the servants who were already beginning to be less plentiful at the turn of the century. His houses are dignified but warm and intimate, with lots of oak panelling. In the 1890s, Brierley immersed himself in the growing programme of school building that followed from Forster's famous Education Act of 1870. Of his three impressive schools in York, Scarcroft Road is probably his masterpiece. It was planned for 1,260 pupils aged 5 to 14 and was to have 21 classrooms with about 60 pupils per class. It is an enormously practical building with ample accommodation for things like store-rooms and cloakrooms fitted into corner pavilions and on mezzanine levels – the kind of essentials often left out. Meticulous attention was paid to details – sloping brick windowsills in the classrooms; patterning of two kinds of brick on the exterior; original door-locks and handles; a klaxon for a fire alarm; bookcases fitted in to partitions between hall and classroms; fitted attendance blackboards by the doors; and a complicated heating system worked by a huge coal boiler and an engine that blew hot air around, with ducts to suck air in and fumes out on the corner towers. The plan is deceptively simple with an enormous central hall, top lit and ventilated by louvres on strings. Off this opens all the classrooms. There are two symmetrical wings projecting at each end of this main rectangular block, and square towers reaching up in each of the four re-entrant angles, three with cupolas and one with the chimney from the boilerhouse.

and 1911 (and thereafter as Professor in the Royal College of Art) he brought together in a way that has never been followed since the designers and makers of artefacts and the designers of buildings. His own houses belong to the Arts and Crafts Movement. His church at Brockhampton incorporates the main features of the movement and its demise; for it has a thatched roof resting on top of a concrete roof structure – the vernacular protecting modern engineering.

What, to summarize, did all these designers offer? They had been inspired by their study of the vernacular more than any aristocratic style, to produce what Muthesius called *Das Englische Haus*. Its characteristics were the living hall, from which other rooms opened, the great fireplace with its open hearth and inglenooks and interior spaces through the house whose volumes interpenetrated through wide doors or arches. The garden was linked with the house and integrated with it – not as completely as we shall see in Chapter Five when Frank Lloyd Wright took the potential in these English houses to its most complete expression. In short, the architecture inspired by the vernacular was a total

design, of all things from the whole house and its cottages and gates and outhouses and fences down to the knives and forks. It was a free architecture and it seemed to be part of the rustic landscape, growing out of it as an extension of Nature.

Not surprisingly, at a time when domestic designs were widely published and exhibitions were mounted in many countries, the same use of the vernacular could be seen in the United States. There, however, the tradition was not that of the English village and the rustic house but that of the prairie house and homestead.

Of the architects using that tradition as the generator of an original style, the most senior was H. H. Richardson who, as we have seen, was trained for a time at the Beaux Arts in Paris but rejected the neo-Classicism of his training. He was obsessed with the indigenous architecture of America. Nor was he alone. The massive masonry of his houses and the unification of the houses with their sites was echoed by other architects and realized most notably in the spreading suburbia to which Lloyd Wright was to make the most dramatic contribution.

The most complete expression of this was in California where

Christian Science Church, Berkeley, California: Bernard Maybeck (1909–11)

Maybeck was a contemporary of F. L. Wright's and had studied at the Ecole des Beaux Arts in Paris in the 1880s. This church presents the tantalizing bridge between two architectural worlds typical of the period. It has a traditional ceremonial axis, but a concrete structure. It uses concrete, asbestos and even industrialized parts, but also carved wood, close-set mullions of small glass panes, and lots of wisteria which looks like part of the design. As with Greene and Greene's architecture, both Japanese and log cabin influences can be seen in the stickwork and the weird collection of jutting roofs, facing in different directions.

(Opposite)

Gamble House, Pasadena, California: Charles and Henry Greene (1908–9)

In the first 15 years of the 20th century, the distinctive form of the American Arts and Crafts Movement crossed to the west coast with architects like Maybeck and the Greene brothers. Their new architecture was to overthrow the Spanish Mission revival style currently in vogue in the west. Their work drew on varied influences – English Arts and Crafts, West Coast vernacular, Swiss, Scandinavian and American cabins, and the Japanese wooden tradition. Many of these were illustrated in a magazine called *The Craftsman* published between 1901 and 1916. The Greene brothers had trained in woodwork at Calvin Woodward's Manual Training School in St Louis in the 1870s, and

then at Massachusets Institute of Technology at Boston. They prided themselves as architect-craftsmen, and liked to work on the site, not merely supervising, but personally working on wooden details.

The Gamble House, built for Proctor and Gamble, the soap people, is now the home of the Greene and Greene Society. In it, the traditional Californian bungalow came of age as a Great House. The plan is simple. The core is the English living hall, here lying between terraces to back and front. Japanese stick architecture is used on the balconies which contain sleeping porches.

Many internal features are in lovingly-polished maple. The actual redwood structure of the house is exposed: we can see how each bit fits together as in those traditional Japanese structures that were originally designed to be taken down and put together again to suit the movements of a peripatetic court. Dove-tailing, pegging together with

square dowels, sliding joints with pegs and thongs against earthquakes – all are open to inspection. The house is a veritable museum of craftsmanship.

(Above)

Glessner House, 1800 South Prairie Avenue, Chicago: Henry Hobson Richardson (1886)

Richardson built three large houses this year, one in St Louis and two in Chicago, all using his typical monumental masonry. Henry-Russell Hitchcock calls his house for J. J. Glessner 'almost as perfect a domestic paradigm of granite construction as the Pittsburgh Jail.' Instead of setting his house well back, American fashion, on the ample site, Richardson built his frontage along the street line, to allow an enclosed courtyard for carriages and extra private space at the back.

with plenty of land and not too much imported tradition, the large vernacular house was a natural development. After training in the East, the brothers Greene, Charles (1868–1957) and Henry (1870–1954), moved to California and developed a regional style there based upon the indigenous use of timber and their own knowledge of joinery, including Japanese. They were trained as craftsmen in wood and maintained that role throughout their architectural work.

Their most celebrated work, now a national monument, was the Gamble House of 1907–8, in effect a Californian bungalow on a great scale built for a millionaire from the soap firm Procter & Gamble. The brothers designed and supervised every detail, making changes on site during construction. It is the most intimate and friendly house revealing at every point the care taken in detail, like the sliding joints devised to allow the house to move in the event of earthquakes. It is the joinery that surpasses – redwood frames and beams, olive-green shakes or shingles on the roof. With that went stained-glass panels in the windows, Tiffany lights. The main space, as in the English houses, becomes the link to all the others.

Did the use of the vernacular have to contribute lastingly to the architecture of the 20th century? There were problems that it never fully resolved of which two were fundamental. Like the Arts and Crafts Movement, of which it is in effect a constituent, it never found out how to use the local native vernacular cheaply, for the unprivileged for whom the vernacular was provided. And it never solved the problem for the architect of needing to be on the spot throughout construction and modifying details – possibly only if there was plenty of money and time.

What it did offer lastingly was freedom, a return to Nature, something personal and local and speaking of local culture. And it grew from small to big – the detail of a piece of jewellery leading if explored with imagination to an understanding of space. Of that understanding the most outstanding exponent was Charles Rennie Mackintosh, to whom we now turn.

CHAPTER FOUR

SPATIAL UNDERSTANDING

Charles Rennie Mackintosh was born in Glasgow in 1868, the second of the eleven children of a Glasgow policeman. He was articled to the architect John Hutchinson at the age of 16 and attended evening classes at Glasgow School of Art. In 1884 he joined the firm of Honeyman and Keppie. He was a frequent winner of architectural prizes, travelled in Italy, delivered a number of papers to Glasgow architects. Then in 1896, still working for Honeyman and Keppie, Mackintosh won the competition for a new Glasgow School of Art. It was an event celebrated locally at the time. It was to become one of the greatest monuments of modern architecture in Europe.

Mackintosh's reputation spread as a result of two articles in *The Studio* in 1897 devoted to 'Some Glasgow Designers'. In particular the articles dealt with the work of the group described as 'The Four'. They were Mackintosh, his friend Herbert McNair and the sisters Margaret and Frances Macdonald. Mackintosh married Margaret and McNair married Frances, shortly afterwards setting off for Liverpool where he taught Decorative Design. They were collectively nicknamed by the editor of *The Studio* as 'the Spook School'. Directly influenced by Art Nouveau, they produced designs for posters and illustrations, decorative plaques, clocks and mirrors and furniture – tables, settees, cabinets and cupboards – with features with swinging lines and whiplash curves, tendrils and drops, with beads of coloured glass and hard enamel surfaces. Where was the origin for this decorative school? It was, as we have already seen, Nature, especially the danker, more wet and mysterious aspects of Nature, like pools and mists and drooping trees, that inspired the phrase 'spook school'.

The key to Mackintosh's bigger designs for such as the Art School can be found by studying his furniture. Its link with Nature was not only in decorative finishes. He noted that in Nature plants are grouped in irregular ways and have different heights; so the furniture in a room – in marked contrast with what was to happen later in the Modern Movement – should have different heights, tall

chairs and lower ones, different heights and dimensions of tables to suit their need. He measured up some of his clients to make sure the furniture was suitable for them.

Some of the furniture, like the famous ladder-back hall chair, was frankly decorative, not intended for ordinary use but as a three-dimensional decorative object that could also serve to hold things if necessary. Others, like the card table for four people, was almost obsessively functional with its square top surface for the cards and the lower levels at the corners for holding tea cups while the game progressed. In short his furniture revealed what, on a smaller scale, his jewellery had done – his fascination with forms, interpenetrating in three dimensions. When turning a piece of jewellery in the hand, it is seen from different sides and Mackintosh applied this principle to his architectural designs. A fascinating and changing complex of forms seen behind and through others unfolded. Here was a magic, offered by Nature if it were studied, so simple that it could be achieved without artificiality by the imaginative use of materials needed in any case for functional reasons, and without needing historical detail. All it needed was the right kind of vision, the ability to visualize interpenetrating space – spatial understanding.

That may sound simple but it has not been characteristic of many architects and styles of architecture. It was probably at its most vivid and richest in the period of the Baroque and Rococo, with complex geometric shapes providing a wonderful opportunity for dramatic lighting and colour. For some reason which I do not fully understand, it became central to designs around the turn of the century. Mackintosh was not alone in possessing this gift; contemporaries designing churches in late Gothic style revealed it; Lutyens, as we shall see, had it to a quite exceptional degree. But,

Murals from Buchanan Street Tearooms, Glasgow: Charles Rennie Mackintosh (1896)

Mackintosh re-modelled the premises for Miss Catherine Cranston. The interior design and furniture was by George Walton. Mackintosh contributed a series of Art Nouveau figures surrounded by tendrils of climbing roses that are stencilled all round the walls of the dining-room, dinner gallery and smoking gallery. These figures are so spaced as to resemble caryatids carrying the cornice. The interiors were later altered when the building became a bank.

increasingly, Mackintosh is recognized as the architect of space *par excellence*.

To take some of his best buildings (not in chronological order), it is obvious in the designs for Miss Cranston's Tearooms, where he designed everything from the wall frescoes and furniture and interiors to the knives and forks – fascinating views between the balusters of galleries to the frescoes and vertical patterns below. It is more dramatic and possibly at its most sensitive in his houses. The finest house – and some people think his finest work – was Hill House in Helensburgh of 1902–3.

Hill House is simple and plain almost to the point of ugliness outside, a pair of austere blocks linked at right angles, with a few features caused entirely by the need to make a different kind of interior. And that interior is a feast of imaginative design – basically simple, wholly original, endlessly inventive. There are fine practical touches, like the sash windows that can be cleaned from the inside and the slots in the end of the arms of the window seat to hold books. The hall is dark and narrow. But the main bedroom is often considered one of the set pieces of architectural

Queen's Cross Church, 866 Garscube Road, Glasgow: C. R. Mackintosh (1897–9)

Built for the Church of Scotland and now the premises of the Mackintosh Society, the church stands at a busy junction in an area much opened up in recent years by tenement demolition. Mackintosh started work on these designs immediately after the competition designs for the School of Art. He designed the church, exterior stonework carving, the glass, the oak pulpit, the communion table, three chairs and a cabinet. The plan is traditional for the Church of Scotland as it has a gallery, but more unusual features – the fruit of Mackintosh's habit of sketching obsessively wherever he went – can be noted. The staircase to the gallery is unusual, and, according to his biographer, Tom Howarth, the battered tower with engaged turret is based on a church at Merriot, Somerset.

Hill House, Helensburgh, Dumbartonshire (entrance front and south front): C. R. Mackintosh (1902–3)

Built for Walter Blackie the publisher, the house stands on the hillside above the town and overlooks the end of the Gareloch and the Clyde estuary. The material is local sandstone, rendered in whitish harling.

Elevations show the strongly Scottish Baronial character of its massing, gables, chimneys and turret – built to stand proud against the assaults of the elements. Mackintosh designed everything including the garden in meticulous detail: he even left instructions as to how bushes were to be clipped.

(Opposite, below)

Hill House – Hall

Hill House interiors use typical Mackintosh contrasts of light and dark, offset here and there by vivid studs of pink or blue or purple or green, often of glass set into wooden panels. He designed everything inside – the decoration, fireplaces, furniture, built-in fittings, details down to pewter fireirons. The entry hall is quite small, but, as in the School of Art entry and library, gives a magical sense of interpenetrating spaces, due to his manipulation of levels both of floor and ceiling, and chequerboard patterns of light and dark achieved by cutting away squares from screens and furniture.

Hill House – Drawing Room

This room is mainly white with a darker polished floor and (now) a black ceiling. Wide horizontal casements flood it with light over the famous window seat with its slots designed for the owner to slip his open book into, should his reading be disturbed by visitors. A delicate pale rose motif is stencilled round the walls.

Hill House – Main Bedroom

Some think this to be one of the world's most perfect rooms. It has three functional areas – for sitting, dressing and sleeping. It faces south over the garden and down to the loch, and is almost entirely white, so that occupants wake to an atmosphere sufficiently airy to make them feel quite light-headed about life. There is built-in furniture round the bed in the sleeping alcove. The high ladder-backed chairs are not designed for sitting on: there is a special built-in couch by the fireside to curl up on.

history. Mackintosh shaped a single room so that it could be seen as distinct spaces – for sleeping, for sitting, for dressing. So the ceiling is shaped above the bed alcove; the full length mirrors define the dressing area.

'The power,' he said in a lecture about 1900, 'which the artist possesses of representing objects to himself explains the hallucinating character of his work – the poetry which pervades them – and their tendency towards symbolism – but the creative imagination is far more important. The artist cannot attain to mastery in his art unless he is endowed in the highest degree with the faculty of invention.'

That would of course be true for artists of many ages. But Mackintosh was quite clear about the specific character of the art – and thus the architecture – of his own time. It is central to the argument of this book. 'The only true modern individual art in proportion in form and in colour, is produced by an emotion, produced by a frank and intelligent understanding of the abolute and true requirement of a building or object – a scientific knowledge of the possibilities and beauties of material, a fearless application of emotion and knowledge, a cultured intelligence, and a mind artistic yet not too indolent to attempt the task of clothing in grace and beauty the new forms and conditions that modern development of life – social, commercial and religious – insist upon.'

That could stand as a manifesto for the modern movement as understood at the time – and today. Like Gaudi, Mackintosh was well read and familiar with contemporary art theory. Indeed he plagiarized Lethaby in a lecture given in 1893, drawing from Lethaby's book *Architecture, Mysticism and Myth* and explaining his approach precisely. 'Architecture,' he said, 'is the synthesis of the fine arts, the commune of all the crafts.'

But ultimately it is one great building that gave Mackintosh the opportunity to bring together all his knowledge and understanding, not only of space but of the commune of the crafts, and to do so in a truly organic way that also has an important lesson for today. As I have already said, he won the competition for the Glasgow School of Art in 1896. The Principal of the School, Francis Newberry, knew the work of The Four and no doubt influenced the decision of the judges. He also protected Mackintosh throughout the design of the building and its erection. Like Hill House, it is almost distressingly plain on the outside, big windows for studios on the north and an elevation that is not even symmetrical. It was built in two main stages and the difference between the two effectively sums up Mackintosh's architectural development. The building is now so well known as to need no description. It reveals the genius with which Mackintosh did what Lutyens did not – making a poetic statement out of a relatively big

Glasgow School of Art, 167 Renfrew Street, Glasgow: C. R. Mackintosh (1897–9, 1907–9)

Mackintosh designed the School of Art when working for the firm of Honeyman and Keppie, one of eight architectural firms invited by the College Governors to enter designs for a new building in a limited competition. It was built in two phases for financial reasons, and Mackintosh made changes as work progressed, a method that suited his way of working and was in accord with his belief that an architect's original design should be accepted as his intention, not something fixed and unalterable. Thus, in the second phase, extra staircases were added to satisfy fire regulations, and a row of masters' studios added as an attic floor. The rectangular site slopes down to the city centre. In accordance with competition prescriptions that it should be plain, it is built of ashlar stone with some brick, the façade cut and sculpted rather than decorated. The entry front on the north is composed of ranges of giant horizontal windows which light the studios. Railings, an entry bow arch with lamp, and rose-finished supports for window cleaning-planks to give cleaners access to the windows are original Mackintosh ironwork. The west front where the hill falls away below the building is less aggressive, beautifully modelled with slim vertical bands of small-mullioned windows patterning one side of the elevation.

building. He did so by the simplest of devices, the minimum of grandeur and the maximum of originality.

The plan of the School of Art is, after all, so simple as to be elementary. Lutyens would have been ashamed of it. There are studios along the north, corridors and ducts along the south, and the library on the west. It was not only simple, it was also organic. The later stairs were cut away to clear windows formerly on the outside. The 'hen run' on the top was an afterthought to link it all together.

But out of that very simple, rectilinear plan – and by using only the same simple rectilinear themes – he creates a whole forest of light and shade and fantasy. In the words of another of his lectures plagiarizing Lethaby, 'We must clothe modern ideas with modern dress – adorn our designs with living fancy.'

The wrought-iron brackets to the studio windows are famous for their fanciful elaboration upon a practical need, for structural stability and practical utility. Let me only look at three places – the main stair, the south stair and the library. The first is a study in thick and thin, straight and tapering verticals, in square chequers, in timber members overlapping, holding and clasping each other and forming a total structure; the south stair, too, is a quite brilliantly imaginative exploitation of the simplest of functional components – a flat floor projected through the opening to end in a curve, with another curve as a balustrade on top of it, a similar curve in another plane below it to support it, and still another at right angles to act as a stiffener. The library is yet another exercise in simplicity, this time in post and beam construction, adding up to a total fantastic grove which is not only designed with a three-dimensional imagination but has to be experienced in three dimensions, looking across and through and up and down.

Both inside and out, the library is Mackintosh at his most personal and expressive. After some more tearooms and minor works on houses he left Glasgow in 1914 and in 1923 settled in the South of France where he produced the most exquisite watercolours before returning to England to die in 1928. In some ways, therefore, his life was tragic. In other ways a triumph. When he visited Vienna in 1900 for an exhibition of his work he was carried shoulder high through the streets by architectural students. He was in his own time recognized by architects in many countries more than his own. By now his reputation, which was small until after the Second World War, is assured – for today's architectural students, the School of Art is as necessary a building to visit and study as the Parthenon or Chartres were for earlier generations.

What they have to study in his mastery of three dimensions, his spatial understanding. In the library he was able to use simple rods and planes, shallow curves, straight lines and squares and

Interior: C. R. Mackintosh

The basic, regular, E-shaped plan takes on in actuality a quirky, asymmetrical character of exciting spatial contrasts and progressions, not only horizontally but in an upward movement of space from level to level.

(Above)
Studios: C. R. Mackintosh

The studios are lofty white rooms, their height emphasized by giant easels designed by Mackintosh. The architect made a virtue out of shortage of money for the project and deliberately eschewed any finer finishings in the studios. He exposed plates and rivets on steel and iron structural members, and left timber roughly sawn-off, cement rendering unfinished. The atmosphere is possessed by the raw smell of materials and an exciting robustness as of sleeves just rolled up.

(Opposite, above)
Library: C. R. Mackintosh

Due to Mackintosh's interplay of spaces and variations of planes in both horizontal and vertical elements and his wonderful manipulation of light, from photographs one presumes the library to be larger than it is. He uses verticals, horizontals and gentle curves in timber to work out a richly decorative space, defined and shaped by columns, beams, cover plates and hanging frets. Eight foot wide galleries run along the upper part of the room, and beyond these, a further four feet out into the room, stand the giant columns which support the roof; the space between gallery rail and these columns is bridged by fretwork banisters. These columns, the verticals on the galleries and the bead-curtain of light chains hanging from the roof, all serve to give the impression of a forest of slim verticals and make the room seem unusually high; in fact, it is half the height of the studios below. As with all the best works of art, there seem to be no end to the magic effects and exciting finds to be made in a relatively small room only 35 feet square. One has, for instance, to walk right into the window embrasure and look up to discover that one is standing in a hexagonal funnel in which the window mullions on one side and the chequered woodwork on the other form a reversal pattern of light on dark/dark on light.

(Opposite, below)
Boardroom: C. R. Mackintosh

Mackintosh not only designed interesting windows and light fittings, but was in advance of his time in designing how light should fall from light sources. Like the Director's Office, this room is painted white even to the steel beams which support the ceiling – white panelling, white woodwork, white light contrasting with the strong geometrical planes and bold linear forms of the furniture which has been collected from various sources to make this something of a showroom for Mackintosh furniture, glass, paintings, watercolours, ironwork and light fittings.

SOUTH ELEVATION

chequers, a vocabulary of simple, fundamental elements to create the magic, the poetry which he called for in the lecture quoted above. In Chicago, Louis Sullivan was to produce an equal excitement from more elaborate decorative work but even greater simplicity of the whole. Few architects seem to have such a unique mastery of visualizing three-dimensional space.

In what does it consist? It is the ability to see space almost as if the lines and planes were transparent thereby allowing the architect to imagine the spaces or volumes running through and out of each other and meeting. One way to describe it is as though the designer visualizes spaces as solids and designs *them*, finally enclosing them or enveloping the air.

To achieve this effect Mackintosh employed again and again the simplest of forms – straight lines grouped closely together in parallel, simple, rectangular planes meeting or retreating from them, patterns of square chequers either as flat patterns on a wall or as spars with open spaces between them and occasional shallow curves in one, two or three dimensions. The spaces thus do in fact interpenetrate and are seen to do so. Every space is an adventure leading to another space and another adventure. In the

Liverpool Cathedral Competition Drawing, South Elevation: C. R. Mackintosh (1903)

Lethaby and Edward Prior also submitted entries to this competition, which was won by Giles Gilbert Scott. Mackintosh retained the traditional vocabulary, not much changed from that of Queen's Cross Church of about six years earlier. The plan is essentially orthodox, the style Art Nouveau. The bold exterior massing of the east end is particularly impressive. So are the flying buttresses. What he would have made of the interior remains one of the most tantalizing might-have-beens of history.

case of the School of Art library the corridor with its windows and conversation seats leads inexorably to the library doors, with the chequers – and then inside is the most complex set of related forms creating a total organic complex, as if elongated and tense forms are in beautiful equilibrium.

That was a triumph, for in the context of this attempt to understand what was happening to architecture it showed that magic could be made from the simplest components – and that lies at the heart of any modern architecture.

CHAPTER FIVE

THE PRINCIPLE OF CONTINUITY

Organic Architecture

The idea of continuity in Nature can be traced at least as far back as Aristotle. But it has recurred at many subsequent phases in history and specifically in the study of Natural History. In the 18th century, it fascinated the philosophers whose influence was crucial to the invention and development of the English Landscape Garden. An architect searching for unity in his formal buildings, such as country houses, might insist on the continuity or consistency of design throughout the house, from big to small; the architects of the great 18th century houses, notably Robert Adam, were also the designers of furniture and fittings and artefacts.

But a more fundamental continuity was discovered and exploited by the landscape gardeners, almost as a natural extension of the unity within the house. The elimination of boundaries by such simple devices as the ha-ha so that the architect, in Kent's words, could 'leap the fence and find all Nature was a garden', created a far greater unity between the house and its site than had been possible before. The Victorian importing of more exotic plant material and the development of the garden room enclosed by glass and rich with plants brought the outdoors within the house.

Now, at the turn of the century, developments in structure and building services made it possible to create a fundamental unity between inside and outside. In that development the most lasting, influential and dramatic figure was Frank Lloyd Wright. To him we must now turn.

His overweening self-confidence, if not conceit, can be gauged by the following communication to Henry Russell Hitchcock. Hitchcock was the man who more or less invented the International Style as a term to give coherence to the great *International Exhibition of Modern Architecture* at the Museum of Modern Art in New York in 1932. Wright was included in that exhibition but indicated his total contempt for the International Style and never failed to insult its practitioners, such as Le Corbusier. He made his position clear from the start to Hitchcock: 'I warn Henry Russell Hitchcock right here and now that, having a good start, not only do I fully intend to be the greatest architect who has yet lived, but the greatest who will ever live. Yes, I intend to be the greatest architect of all time.'

Wright had no doubt that he was a genius. And he was seen as more than just an architect. He was regarded by many of his countrymen as probably the greatest American of his generation. The exhibition of his work in Germany in 1910 made him a European figure and established him as an innovator well in advance of most of the continental architects of his time. By the time of the First World War, when he still had two major phases of design work in front of him, he was already a recognized master whose work, even then, would have been enough to place him in history.

Wright's own life was in any case a journalist's delight. His *Autobiography*, first published in 1932 and revized by himself from time to time, is one of the most exciting books on architecture ever published. It was a life full of tempest and glory in which everything was carried out to the full. In Louis Sullivan's office, in which he spent seven years, his disagreements with other assistants led to fights and even to his being stabbed. His marriages were headline news. Having left his first wife, he fled to Europe for the exhibition with the wife of one of his clients and then came back amid great publicity and set up home in his own Wisconsin. She and their children were murdered by a black servant who went suddenly mad and the house was burned to the ground. The rebuilt house burned down again ten years later. In between those disasters he had a disastrous marriage and then married again. The legal attacks by the lawyers for his second wife and the husband of the third landed him in gaol and brought about his bankruptcy, from which he was rescued only by setting himself up as a company and persuading former clients to take shares in him. He was as conceited, as volatile and as impossible as it is possible to be.

But he was a great architect. In his approximately 90 years – approximately, because there is some doubt about the date of his birth and he told different stories about it – he brought into architecture many features that we now take for granted. He developed the open plan, he was a pioneer in air conditioning, in under floor heating, in the use of concrete, in fabrics and textiles, in structural engineering. From his own comments it is clear that he was the sole inventor of all these things. Others might disagree. And the same problem applies to the style of his buildings for on his architectural influences he was remarkably coy. The only architectural source we can go to for a start is Sullivan, and

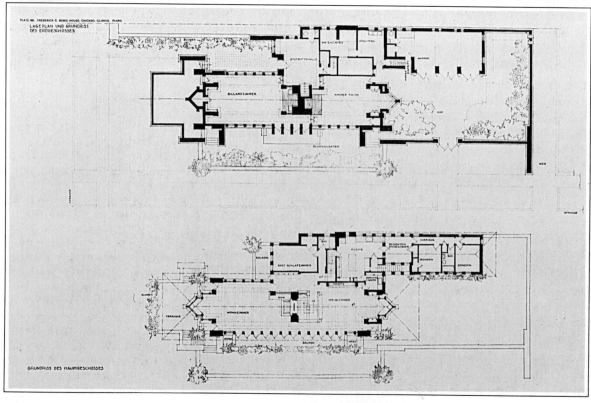

PLATE 88. FREDERICK C. ROBIE HOUSE, CHICAGO, ILLINOIS. PLANS

LAGEPLAN UND GRUNDRISS
DES ERDGESCHOSSES

GRUNDRISS DES HAUPTGESCHOSSES

enquire who had influenced *him*. For Wright, Sullivan was the 'Lieber Meister' from whom he learned his art. Sullivan had been trained as an architect (though not for very long). He had been admitted to the Ecole des Beaux Arts and learned his mastery of the styles both there and in America. His autobiography, *The Autobiography of an Idea*, is at first compulsive reading and then trails away into pages about Democracy. But there are at least two significant aspects of his thought that profoundly influenced Wright.

The first was the slogan for which Sullivan has become famous. It came to him as a sudden truth; he had found, in his own words, 'a universal law admitting of no exception in any phase or application whatsoever.' That was the slogan, 'Form Follows Function'. In fact, as Sullivan records it, he had discovered from his studies of nature and the sciences that it was not simply a matter of form expressing function; the fact was that 'the function created or organized its form'. Discernment of this idea threw a vast light upon all things within the universe; the application of the idea to the architectural art was that the function of a building must predetermine and organize its form.

There are only certain moments in the history of architectural theory when a principle suddenly gets stated in such a way that it can never again be ignored whether or not it is wholly true. This was one of them. It has had a profound influence, disastrous usually because people have not properly studied and understood the function and built upon the most superficial understanding of it.

The second aspect of Sullivan's work, which appears at first to conflict with the first, was that he was a superb decorative artist. His office used Owen Jones' *Grammar of Ornament* and developed its own system of ornament. Sullivan worked upon and elaborated the most intricate decorative systems for his buildings, sometimes as flat applied decoration, increasingly (and supremely in his masterpiece the Carson Pirie and Scott Store in Chicago) as three-dimensional panels made of cast iron.

Where did he find his inspiration? In the same way as the better-known artists of Art Nouveau, he found it in nature, in forms growing and shifting and intertwining, displaying the great principle of Continuity. It was this that Wright was to build upon.

Wright did not go to a school of architecture. His formidable mother had given him a training in Froebel's educational system, which probably helps to explain his superb understanding of three-dimensional form. He then went not to a school of architecture but to the University of Wisconsin where he studied civil engineering, and, in his own words, was 'spared the curse of the architectural education of that day in the US with its false direction in culture and wrong emphasis on sentiment.' Instead,

Robie House. 577 Woodlawn Avenue, Chicago: Frank Lloyd Wright (1909)

The 'Oak Park years' were the first phase of Wright's architectural practice. The many houses designed by him for a Chicago suburb were to revolutionize the American house, and prove internationally seminal. About the influences on his own style, Wright was remarkably coy. At the end of his autobiography he appended a brief bibliography of the works that he had 'long consulted and occasionally remembered'. He mentions Pythagoras, Aristotle, Buddha, Jesus, Tolstoy, William Blake, Walt Whitman, Thoreau, Goethe, Neitsche, Shakespeare and Major Douglas, the inventor of Social Credit. But he does not list a single writer on architecture. The only architect he mentions is Louis Sullivan, and he insists that he had not read Sullivan's writings on the grounds that Sullivan had been an open book to him for years. A climax was the house in the centre of Chicago, not within the University, known as the Robie House.

Robie House – plan

The Robie House is in rich, earthy, Roman brick and lies in one long low axis pressed along mother earth and pegged down in the centre by the hearth core to the house. The overlapping horizontal planes of roof, walls and plinth resemble shifting layers of geological strata. But the image critics have most frequently applied is that of a bi-plane, newly landed. Vincent Scully so describes the source of its power to catch the imagination: 'The two persistent American images, the first of mobility – of flight, of "getting away" – the second of rootedness and security are now locked together in one climactic work that culminates a century or more of American art.'

Avery Coonley House, 300 Scottswood Road, Riverside, Illinois: Frank Lloyd Wright (1908)

This is another of Wright's 'prairie' houses. A pool beside the terrace reflects the central block from which two wings project. The 'functional zones' Wright spoke of in his houses are clear here: the living room occupies the central block, one wing houses dining and kitchen services and the other the sleeping arrangements. The exposed woodwork of structure and interior furnishing – roof beams, stairwell, banisters, etc, lock together like a Chinese puzzle. In later buildings, Wright formed external geometrical patterns with concrete blocks; only in this house does he use coloured ceramic tiles to decorate the exterior. Four years later, he built the Coonley Playhouse on the estate, on a cruciform plan as classically symmetrical as the Villa Rotonda. The projecting concrete roof slabs are slatted so that light slants through to the levels below. The leaded windows which Wright often used, here adopt the fun theme in a rainbow arrangement of circles of glass – whirling turning circles in the sun.

he discovered the excitement of mathematics. And he had an unforgettable experience when, passing by the new north wing of the old State Capitol, he saw the building collapse and people horrifically killed. 'The horror of the scene,' he said writing of himself, characteristically in the third person, 'never entirely left his consciousness and remains to prompt him to this day.'

Wright's output was phenomenal. He had designed over 140 houses by 1910 (when he exhibited in Europe), as well as at least 50 other structures; and that was only the first phase of his work. On his return from Europe he entered upon another phase of great energy. By the late 1920s he was already an old master. He then started an even more spectacular career and never stopped. In the years after the Second World War, by then in his seventies and eighties, he produced some of his most adventurous structures.

The centre for his first period – that of the 'prairie houses' – was Chicago, especially the suburb of Oak Park, where Wright built his first house for himself and his first studio. In Chicago itself, the most mature example is the Robie House of 1909, now sur-rounded by the University of Chicago, sitting beside a road and less big than the photographs suggest. Earlier designs were the Martin House in Buffalo of 1904 for one of his best clients (Martin helped to bail him out later when he was broke), and the Coonley House of 1908 in Riverside, Illinois. The latter was thought by Wright to be 'the most successful of my houses from my standpoint.' The Martin House had taken to its fullest expression his integration of the house and the landscape, the inside and the outside conceived as one.

What Wright reckoned to have achieved with these houses and what made them distinctive were the following. He broke down the walls as the definitors of the plan, opening up the corners so that houses would no longer be composed of boxes beside or within boxes. What now unified the houses were long sloping roofs with huge overhangs. Light came not from holes in the walls but from continuous strips of windows opening outwards, with patterned leaded lights and hidden sources of natural light. He thus developed the open plan, in which spaces flow one into another, exploiting changes of level and the heights of rooms to create the differentiation of spaces. The main fireplace, the hearth in the literature of the ancient world that he read and admired, became the fulcrum around which the whole plan revolved and then spread out into the garden. To make the whole of this continuous space comfortable he invented (he said) underfloor heating. It was, in his words, the 'uncluttered house' and its virtues were 'organic simplicity' and 'organic plasticity'. The word Organic, he said in a later lecture, means part-to-whole-as-whole-is-to-part; it was a source of unity and reflected what happened in natural growth.

The scale of these houses is unexpected. Wright was not a tall man and that may have influenced him. But in any case it was an organic part of the open plan that the ceiling should be lower than usual except for special areas. The lighting, therefore, became a strip below the ceiling running right round the house protected by the oversailing roof.

In one of his Princeton Lectures of 1930 entitled *The Cardboard House* (other people's house of course) Wright listed the principles that enabled him to put to work the ideal of organic simplicity in these early houses. They were, to abbreviate:

First – To reduce the number of necessary parts of the house and to separate rooms to a minimum, and make all come together as enclosed space – so divided that light, air and vista permeated the whole with a sense of unity.

Second – To associate the building as a whole with its site by extension and emphasis of the planes parallel to the ground.

Third – To eliminate the room as a box and the house as another by making all walls enclosing screens.

Fourth – To get the unwholesome basement up out of the ground, entirely above it, as a low pedestal for the living portion of the home.

Fifth – To harmonize all necessary openings to 'outside' or to 'inside' with good human proportions and make them occur naturally . . . there were to be no holes cut in walls as holes are cut in a box, because this was not in keeping with the ideal of 'plastic'.

Sixth – To eliminate combinations of different materials in favour of mono-material so far as possible; to use no ornament that did not come out of the nature of materials.

Seventh – To incorporate all heating, lighting, plumbing so that these systems became constituent parts of the building itself.

Eighth – To incorporate as organic architecture – so far as possible – furnishings, making them all one with the building and

Ninth – Eliminate the decorator.

If the houses established the character of the spaces and plans that changed domestic architecture forever, it was Wright's engineering ability and structural imagination that marked the next two phases. Between 1916 and 1922 he designed, and had in effect to act as coordinating contractor, the Imperial Hotel in Tokyo.

To counteract the effect of the earthquakes to be expected in Tokyo and despite all the misgivings of his clients and advisers, he devized a structure so that the building would rest on a huge

Martin House, Buffalo, New York: Frank Lloyd Wright (1904)

The house has a typical Wright plan based on the crossing of axes. The extension of these axes into the garden form other contained shapes, providing a single spatial experience through the interpenetration of interior and exterior shapes. Wright's exceptional understanding of three-dimensional geometry, which supports his claim to be the originator of the open plan, was probably instilled in him in his early education at a Froebal kindergarten.

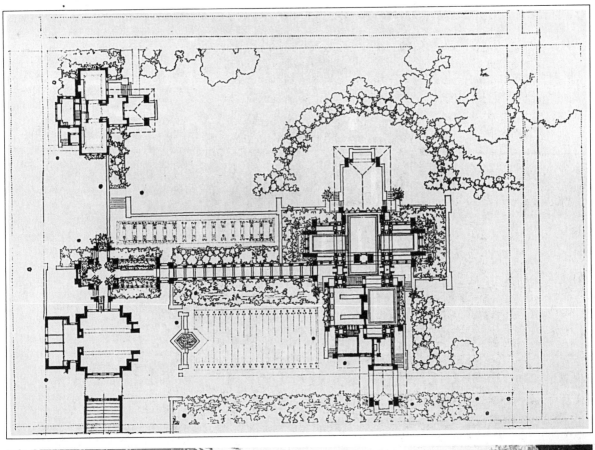

Imperial Hotel, Tokyo: (Frank Lloyd Wright 1916–22)

Neither of the two big works of Wright's so-called 'Baroque' period, the Midway Gardens on the Midway, south of Chicago (1913–14) and the Imperial Hotel, Tokyo are still standing. In neither case does 'Baroque' seem an accurate label for their rough, chunky fantasy. Midway Gardens, a nightclub complex with outside and inside dining, stage and orchestra shed, had also a covered restaurant building in Lowland Mayan temple style, a solid massed outline broken by stick towers of whimsical Japanese derivation at either end of the roof and cubist decorations inside. We know from such buildings as the German Warehouse at Wisconsin of 1915, directly copied from the Temple of the Two Lintels at Chichen Itza, that Wright was prepared to borrow Mayan details wholesale. The Midway Gardens was destroyed by prohibition. There was Aztec and Mayan blocking and carving all over the Imperial Hotel, too, but the rough stonework (some in greenish lava) and jutting cornerstones and lintels speak more of Hindu temples or the aggressive Mannerism of Giulio Romano than of the Baroque. The Hotel was commissioned by the Imperial household in 1915, during the First World War. The plan is H-shaped – a group of related courtyards with spaces opening into one another, its structure wholly and brilliantly original.

concrete raft with a grid of piles, the whole lying on eight feet of cheese-like soil that overlay liquid mud. With the concrete pins positioned at two feet centres over the whole area for the wall footings, he had a good foundation for the superstructure. But what he did with that was even more original. The main walls became not just perimeter walls with floors slung between them but structural spines with the floors cantilevered from them on each side, meeting in the middle of the floor.

The Imperial Hotel was completed in 1922. The great earthquake that destroyed much of Tokyo in 1923 left the Hotel undamaged – he never ceased to publish the famous telegram that told him the hotel had survived 'as monument of your genius'. But essentially the Imperial Hotel revealed an important point about him as an architect and engineer. The structure was not made without calculation for a huge number were made as the bearing power of the soil was tested. More importantly though, it was the first major example of Wright's understanding of structure as a three-dimensional balance of forces. He described the walls as being like a waiter carrying two trays or a tree with branches cantilevered from the trunk. It was, in short, a visual understanding that precedes calculation. The mathematics were not the key to design but a check upon its rationality.

And that would be equally true for the house that he subsequently designed and was built between 1935 and '37 at Bear Run in Pennsylvania, probably the most famous private house to

(Opposite)

Falling Water, Bear Run, Connellsville, Pennsylvania: Frank Lloyd Wright (1935–7)

The Kaufmann House was built over a waterfall in the woods of Pennsylvania for the Pittsburg millionaire, Edgar J. Kaufmann. Wright mastered an almost impossible site and created the most vivid example of man-made form

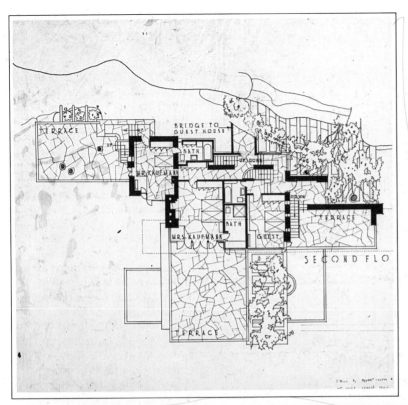

complementing nature. It is probably the most photographed house of the 20th century, although to get the really spectacular views from underneath, it is necessary to wade into the river. The stepped sections of reinforced concrete thrust outwards from the core of masonry to hover in overlapping planes above the rocks, trees and falling water.

Falling Water – plan

The living space is all on one level bounded by stone walls on the dining side, but by walls of glass, set in the least-obtrusive slim metal mullions, on the waterfall side. The rough masonry of the central fireplace which, as in the Robie House, forms the main vertical feature, is complemented by the simple, unornamented concrete cantilevers which form the floors of the house – part inside, part outside – a wholly integrated flow of space from interior to exterior.

be produced in our time. The Kaufmann House, built over a waterfall and known as 'Falling Water,' has concrete cantilevers that form the floor of the house springing from the masonry core, creating a brilliantly integrated flow of space from interior to exterior.

At the same time, Wright played with other materials in the new building for Johnson Wax at Racine. Developing from the cantilevering possibilities of the hotel and the house as well as the materials of an earlier Johnson building, Wright created a tower which is one of his most sophisticated structural ventures – a column with floors cantilevered out from it, alternately square and circular on plan, clad at the perimeter by a curtain wall of glass tubing. The effect of illuminated shapes that cannot be seen behind the glass during the day means that the tower has a different life at night.

On a humbler scale, Wright also developed what he called the Usonian house. He used the word Usonia as a more expressive word than America, specifically in this case to indicate what he saw as the native house for the ordinary American, to be built at low cost. The Usonian house was a simple structure of timber with walls of sandwich construction and flat roofs made of crossed timber scantlings; it took the open plan even further so that the kitchen area became a work-space lit from a clerestory and the house was effectively one space with the minimum of necessary private spaces.

The most attractive and dramatic of the houses designed in the '30s was Taliesin West in the Arizona desert, not far from Phoenix. The name Taliesin is a Welsh word meaning 'shining hill' and Wright built his first Taliesin in his home estate of Wisconsin, a house (in effect a settlement) that grew and changed with its rebuilding after two disastrous fires.

In 1938, Wright began what he called his desert camp and continued to elaborate and change it in a thoroughly organic way until his death in 1959. This was the home and workplace of the Taliesin Fellowship, his school and office that managed to produce not a single great architect from among the many acolytes dominated at first by his presence and later by his recorded voice telling them everything they needed to know about architecture and life. But the buildings are magical. It has a dramatic site, which – like many another such sites – is dramatic because of what he did to it. The main structure is built of what he called desert concrete – huge chunks of rock fixed together in shuttering with as little cement as possible, with sloping sides, an impression of total permanence, elemental in its power.

Wright's last buildings, in the years following the Second World War, were more varied in function and scale than the predominant houses of the earlier years. They included the Unitarian

Johnson Wax Building, 1525 Howe Street, Racine, Wisconsin: Frank Lloyd Wright (1936–9, 1946–9)

This is the administrative building and laboratory tower for S. C. Johnson & Sons. Wright had become interested at this time in Sir Arthur Evans' reconstructions of Minoan palaces at Knossos, Crete, and from this point curves and spirals become important in his buildings. These occur in the main office building at Racine as well as in the later laboratory tower of 1950. Minoan, too, are the spiral-topped, peg-legged columns set in bronze shoes which carry a section of the building on an overhead walkway between two curved blocks. The entrance is underneath the walkway – a feature to be adopted by many office and hotel complexes today.

Johnson Wax Building – interior

The peg-legs are here again, a forest of them, but grown tall and stately to create an open office space below, yet holding up the wide lily-pad discs of concrete that support the roof. The roof is interesting, the middle section being of tubes of Pyrex glass through which comes the light.

Taliesin West, outside Phoenix, Arizona: Frank Lloyd Wright (1938)

Wright spent much of his time here between 1938 and 1959, and died here in this, his winter house, which had come to feel the fulfilment of his ideal. Today, it looks across a wide plain of orange desert and scrubland towards Pheonix, much more built up than it was in Wright's day. It appears to grow out of the desert. The structure above is of redwood, great canted beams and frames filled with canvas so that the whole of an apparently changing interior glows with warm light. The furniture (over whose occupants Wright presided like an inspired prophet) is his own, some of it agonizing to sit on. There are huge fireplaces inside, and outside terraces and pools with great plants that belong to the desert and bring inside and outside together.

church at Madison, Wisconsin (1947–52), using his expressive hands – hands in prayer – and the Price Tower at Battlesville of 1955 which was (at the age of 75) his first multi-storey residential building, with a brilliantly conceived plan of interlocking triangles and squares. Once again the floors are cantilevered out but now form a cruciform spine which holds the dwellings and ends at the top in a geometric terminal of a kind alien to the majority of towers and infinitely better in fashioning a skyline.

His final, and probably best known, major work was the Guggenheim Museum in New York. However, as a precursor of the museum, Wright inserted the Morris Store into a narrow site in the centre of San Francisco. Entering through a meticulously fashioned arched doorway in a blank wall, you suddenly find yourself in a space flooded with light from the roof, with a spiral ramp going up to the roof lined with display cabinets.

Between 1956 and 1959, the housing of the Guggenheim Collection gave Wright the opportunity he had always wanted – to create a major building in New York. He seized it with characteristic determination. The Guggenheim is a spiral enclosed by continuous walls canted outwards, with strips of light between the floors, so that the whole complex is one of the most distinctive

(Opposite, above)

Unitarian Church, Madison, Wisconsin: Frank Lloyd Wright (1947–52)

Both in plan and elevation this church is dominated by a protruding triangle – a great ship's prow cutting its way through the grassy waves of the prairies. As usual with Wright there is a synthesis of several images: the ship is also a plough cutting a furrow through the fecund earth; there is the sheer, sky-aspiring form of the Aztec/Egyptian sacred pyramid; and also the praying hands of Dürer clasped over the congregation.

Unity Church, Oak Park, Chicago: Frank Lloyd Wright (1906)

An early work in the developing style he preferred to call 'Usonian' rather than 'American', it has a classical monumentality of scale from the outside. Wright makes full use of the emotive effect of enclosure and space. The visitor enters under a low entrance and into a dark space, and follows a twisting passage to achieve the open-armed welcome of the church itself. The decor is an integral part of the design, the lines at the corners expressing the changes of space and level. And the whole building is made of concrete – but concrete with a difference. It uses a fine pebble-dash aggregate, carefully poured by Wright to enclose the desired space, producing a much more friendly material than the concrete often seen in Britain.

of all structures in a city not noted for architectural reticence. The only problem is that it is quite unsuitable as a gallery. As one critic put it, now that the Guggenheim trustees have put up a celebrated building by a great (if not the greatest) architect, it only remains for them to erect a separate building to house the pictures.

The scope of Lloyd Wright's work and the succession of phases through which he changed and developed a vast outfit of ideas makes his work a treasure house, not yet exhausted, of ideas about design. He had at least three great gifts – an intimate knowledge of materials, a rare three-dimensional imagination that enabled him to visualize spaces as a continuous, ever stimulating experience, and an understanding of structure rare among architects and even among engineers.

Those gifts enabled him to create an architecture that was, in his word, 'organic'; an architecture that seemed to grow inevitably from the function and the site and was free and continuous enough to unite the inside and the outside and give the whole complex a unity, a unity that seems to grow and is capable of continual change. 'I now propose,' he said early in his autobiography, 'an ideal for the architecture of the Machine Age, for the ideal American building. Let it grow up in that image. The tree.' It is Wright's understanding of Nature, of growth and form, which gives him a uniquely commanding position in the story of modern architecture.

He founded no school of followers even though he had his own school of novices. His real followers were architects like Bruce Goff who looked at Wright's work and went their own way – in Goff's

Solomon R. Guggenheim Museum, New York: Frank Lloyd Wright (1943–6, 1956–9)

This helical concrete building is full of surprises. It is smaller and less dominant on the street line than photographs give one to expect. Unfortunately, there are faults with it as a museum of painting. Wright maintained that the walls should slope out because pictures lean back on an easel as artists paint them which, as anyone who has ever made a painting knows, is nonsense. Wise visitors take the lift to the top and attempt to view the paintings as they descend the spiral. Even that method of viewing has problems: the incline of the spiral is not uniform and the floor therefore gives an impression of heaving beneath the feet; the ramp is not wide enough always to get as far back as one wants without falling over the edge. Nevertheless, there can be no doubt that this is a work of genius. In no other building is the structural form so calmly and indissolubly merged with pure abstract design – a perfect piece of op art.

case using natural materials and industrial waste, as did Gaudi, to create a romantic architecture as expressive as Wright's prairie houses. Particularly eccentric in his use of materials – one igloo-shaped house is built of decreasing circles of Coca-Cola cans – Goff expressed his philosophy thus: 'The usual definition of organic architecture is "that which grows from within outward through the natural use of materials so the form is one with function". However, we must go further, and continue with "as directed and ordered by a creative spirit".'

CHAPTER SIX

POWER AND POETRY

This chapter is dominated by the figure of Edwin Lutyens because the resolution of his place in the development of modern architecture is crucial to its understanding. He does not fit into the conventional story. Yet in his time he was well known, prolific as an architect and celebrated in his own lifetime more than any of his contemporaries. When he died in 1944 he was described as the most distinguished English architect of his generation, as the greatest architect since Wren, and as possibly the greatest architect England had ever produced.

On the other hand, within a few years of his death he was being eliminated from reputable histories of the present day. For instance, he does not receive an entry in a standard Encyclopaedia of Modern Architecture. As Sir Nikolas Pevsner remarks in his *Outline of European Architecture*, 'For the first forty years of this century, no English name in architecture need be mentioned.'

Lutyens was born in London in 1869 – the same year as Charles Rennie Mackintosh in Scotland and, in America, Frank Lloyd Wright (possibly born in 1868). A few years later the Lutyens family moved to Surrey when his father, who was an army officer, retired early to take up painting. They lived in a large house called *The Cottage* where Edwin – the eleventh of fourteen – was surrounded by paintings, horses, dogs and, of course, children. His father was a friend of Landseer, whose surname was given to his godson Edwin as his second name.

Because of illness Edwin did not go to school. Nor, in due course, did he go to a school of architecture but spent two years at what later became the Royal College of Art in Kensington leaving before completing any training. He then worked as an assistant in Sir Ernest George's architectural office for six months before leaving and setting up on his own.

What Lutyens had done was immeasurably more useful to him than had he pursued the more conventional training. He said that illness had afforded him time to think and led him to use his eyes instead of his feet. Instead of going to school or university, he

Munstead Wood, Godalming, Surrey: Edwin Lutyens (1896)

Lutyens' first country house was built for Miss Gertrude Jekyll, the guardian angel with whom he shared a passion for the countryside, and with whom he was to collaborate, she supplying the garden design in many of his commissions for houses. Appropriately, the young architect met Miss Jekyll at a tea party in the house of one Harry Mangles who bred rhododendrons. 'My house,' said Miss Jekyll, 'is to be built for me to live in and love; it is not to be built as an exposition of architectonic inutility.' Writing of the house in *Homes and Garden* in 1900, she says it is 'designed and built in the thorough and honest spirit of the good work of the old days. . . . Everything about it is strong and serviceable and looks and feels as if it would wear and endure for ever. It almost gives the impression of a comfortable maturity of something like a couple of hundred years. . . .' The house is U-shaped with six bedrooms; it is made of local stone, has a red-tiled roof, tall brick chimneys and superbly crafted wooden beams and window-frames in heavy oak. Miss Jekyll's natural and irregular garden incorporated surrounding woodland and great banks of flowers, so arranged to give a massive patchwork of intense colour at all seasons.

Munstead Wood – The Gallery

This is the first appearance of a particularly attractive Lutyens' feature – the upstairs gallery. His use of wood here is particularly happy: if you look at the oak frames, you can judge from the tolerances how well he understood the nature and behaviour of timber, a lively and ever-changing material.

walked through the Surrey countryside, exploring old buildings and watching new ones go up. He went to the village carpenter's shop and the yard of the local builder, learning about wood and stones and metals.

He had the most amazing visual memory. He was said to know St Paul's Cathedral and Stokesay Castle by heart. Just as important, however, was a decision he took at about the age of 14. Having heard a family friend, Dicky Doyle of *Punch*, saying that he drew something every day, Lutyens decided to design something every day. It was a habit that made him inexhaustible in invention.

In 1889 he received his first commission. But what gave his mind and his powers of invention an entirely new turn was meeting a remarkable woman who was effectively the teacher who opened his eyes.

Gertrude Jekyll was nearly 50 years old when she and Lutyens met in about 1890. She was 26 years older than him and the product of a different, sophisticated cultural background. A painter, a craftsman, an expert in gilding, an accomplished pianist, she had sat at the feet of Ruskin and read all his works. More important, finding her eyesight getting worse so that she could no longer do detailed work, she had channelled her knowledge and energy into gardening. 'Bumps' Lutyens called her, 'Mother of all Bulbs'.

For Miss Jekyll, Lutyens made a first essay in design called *The Hut* but it was his work on her new house, Munstead Wood, that gave him the opportunity for his first mature design and marked the start of his reputation. Munstead Wood was finished in 1896, built in sturdy traditional English style, with oak frames and oak trusses and long windows. The landscape is part of the house and the house part of the landscape. And with it all he created a delightful human scale, bringing together the technical needs of the house and creating an original form from the study of the house's activities.

The period between 1890 and 1914 is considered by some historians to have been the richest period in the history of the English country house and it was a wonderful time to be in practice. Lutyens was the most successful of them all. By the time he was 33, by 1902, all the houses on which his reputation as a house architect rests were complete. He had designed them between the ages of 27 when he did Munstead and 33 when he did Little Thakeham and they included Fulbrook, Orchards, Tigbourne Court, Grey Walls, the Deanery Garden, Marshcourt, Homewood and Folly Farm.

There are important characteristics that give these houses a distinctive role in the history of the English house. In Hampshire, Marshcourt, for example, was a bold experiment in the use of

Orchards, Munstead, Surrey: Edwin Lutyens (1897–9)

When Sir Richard Chance saw Munstead Wood, he cancelled the designs that another architect, Halsey Ricardo, was preparing for his new house, and employed Lutyens instead. The house is set in pine and birch woods and has formal gardens trimmed with a walkway which gives a prospect of the Hogs Back. Like Munstead, it uses local stone (Bargate), red brick for the chimneys, red tiles and leaded casements set in oak – all beautiful materials, lovingly treated. The plan at first seems regular, the house running round a square courtyard with the stable block coming off it in the leg of an 'L', and with a continuous eaves line running round both elements. But surprise succeeds surprise as one enters the house through a tall gate cut in the stable block (and under a whimsical Lutyens dormer that is doing precisely nothing), and reaches the free and innovative spaces inside.

(Opposite, below)

Deanery Garden, Sonning, Berkshire: Edwin Lutyens (1901)

Deanery Gardens was built in Berkshire brick and set in an old walled orchard in the Thames Valley for Mr Edward Hudson, the owner of *Country Life*. The balance and contrast of its elements, combined with rustic homely charm, create a

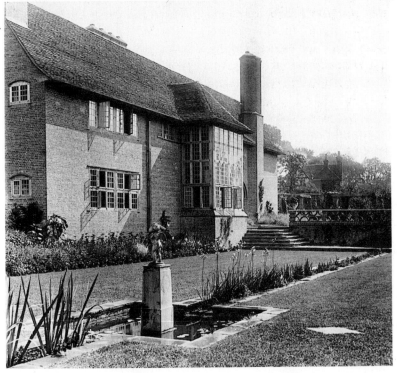

work of unique aesthetic quality, producing a rising excitement followed by the calm peace of resolution and fulfilment. The huge chimneys, one of which relates to the fireplace placed across the corner of the sitting-room, reach up arrogantly to the sky. Beside them is the door, recessed in a series of champfers so as to become three dimensional; its shadow appears to fall, in reverse image, in a flight of concentric semi-circular steps down to a little pool. A relatively thin line from a downpipe marks the doorway's left edge; above it a horizontal window under the eaves links the elements together; and finally a projecting bay window, oak-framed and with leaded lights, runs the full height of the house. In such façades he makes his own private statement about the very meaning of architectural form, leaving us full of admiration at his performance.

materials. Lutyens had always admired the versatility of clunch, that is chalk from the lower beds, which can be hard but at the same time a delight to carve. It was used by Elizabethan and Jacobean architects especially in East Anglia. In Hampshire, Lutyens persuaded his client to let him use it for external walls. The walls are made of clunch and flint with occasional bricks; the effect of weathering has given it a quite individual patina and tremendous character.

Not only is his use of materials unexpected but Lutyens' plans are too. He developed a way of going straight into the house only to find the way blocked by a transverse passage. There is rarely a direct way through. In other cases he makes the entrance twist and turn before access is gained to a living space. The ceilings are often lower than expected and the scale is smaller.

To understand these houses it must be remembered that the period in which he was designing them was the last period when houses were run by lots of servants. The two worlds were not expected to interpenetrate. The army of servants had their own corridors and systems of access; the gentry were dependent on their help but did not want to see them too often. Victorian plans achieved this, often with staggering waste of space. Lutyens did it by sheer ingenuity.

Of that succession of celebrated houses, one of the most

Marshcourt, Kings Somborne, near Stockbridge, Hampshire: Edwin Lutyens (1901–4, extended 1924)

Built near Winchester for Herbert Johnson, this E-shaped Tudor house in the white chalk known as clunch, patched with random blocks and bands of darker flint and tile, is no 'little white house'. Once again, a symmetrical plan deceives us in what we expect of the interior. The ground-floor hall is a rich exercise in what Lutyens called Wrenaissance and highly acceptable as a model of what an interior should be. But the counterpart corridor above it on the first floor is Jacobean timber – the vernacular Lutyens at play with the classical Lutyens. Accommodation still follows the pattern of the 19th-century great house – provision for the pursuits of a country gentleman: gun-room, billiard room, smoking room ('A gentleman should have an occupation,' said Lady Bracknell at satisfying is the Deanery Garden at Sonning on the Thames. It was built for Lutyens' patron Edward Hudson, the owner of *Country Life*, the journal which published Lutyens' work regularly, and the buildings editor of which wrote the first major work on his houses. The Deanery was begun in 1901. He started with an old brick wall enclosing an orchard. Unusually for him he created an axis which runs through the house from the gate in the wall of the old Deanery to the new gardens designed with Miss Jekyll. The elevation of this south wall is one of his most celebrated compositions. Throughout the house and gardens there is a perfect balance of wholly different elements manipulated in three dimensions and brought together by the growing plants that creep across the surfaces.

Hudson became a close friend. Having built the Deanery he could not resist the temptation to buy Lindisfarne Castle on Holy Island, off the coast of Northumberland. The remains of a 16th-century castle, it was partly in ruins and he asked Lutyens to restore it. Lutyens did more. He recast it and virtually rebuilt it, transforming it into the most romantic folly on a spectacularly beautiful headland.

Because of its site, there was not much opportunity to sort out the whole of the landscape. But two years later with another 16th-century castle on an island – Lambay Island off the Irish coast near Dublin – he created what some consider his masterpiece – a house in its setting, the whole environment considered as one. For Lutyens it was the last and fondest of his romantic conceptions.

'A garden scheme', he once said, 'should have a backbone, a

this period), and ample servants' quarters. Like all Lutyens pre-war houses, it is short of bathrooms when big houses still relied on flocks of maids carrying ewers of hot water. The prodigality of circulation space (although something for which he was criticised) undoubtedly imparts the particular airy atmosphere in which he so delighted. 'The lavish space given away in staircases makes me sick with envy' he wrote in gleeful relish to his wife. Marshcourt is now a girls' school.

Grey Walls, Gullane, East Lothian, Scotland: Edwin Lutyens (1900)

The wife of the client, the Rt Hon. Alfred Lyttleton, objected to Lutyens' early designs for a Scottish baronial castle with small windows, and Grey Walls emerged as an English country house built in Scottish materials – rough rubble walling, grey Dutch pantiles, patterned with dots of red tile. The entrance drive leads diagonally across a square courtyard to the door in the corner angle between the wings of the building.

Lindisfarne Castle, Holy Island, Northumberland: Edwin Lutyens (1903)

In his reconstruction of two military forts from the 16th century – Lambay Castle on an island in County Dublin, Ireland, and the castle at Holy Island off Northumberland – Lutyens showed how his fertile imagination could capitalize on a situation to produce spectacular results. On Lambay Island he grouped old and new buildings together by surrounding the gardens with a huge circular wall 700 feet in diameter. Lindisfarne was his second commission for Edward Hudson of *Country Life*. Here he exploited the impressive verticality of the old fort, which shot upwards from a sudden massive rock above the water.

central idea beautifully phrased. Every wall, path, stone and flower should have its relationship to the central idea.' At Lambay he seems to have brought together in a rare perfection the inheritance of the rough symmetrical castle, the richness of planting and the informality of a changing scene with an underlying geometry which gives the whole place an extraordinary certitude and serenity.

In about 1904, Lutyens decided that he wanted a more complete aesthetic ideal – a turning point which drastically altered his place in the architecture of the day. He began to play what he called The High Game. And, as always seemed to happen to him, a splendid opportunity for playing the highest game presented itself.

His client was a Yorkshireman who had made a great deal of money in textiles and wished to build a house in Ilkley. He had a site of four acres on the edge of the town and was a man who, said Lutyens, 'could not spend his money – until he met me.' He got the very opposite of what he asked for and he got it because it gave Lutyens an opportunity to play with the classical orders.

The house is Heathcote. Lutyens decided from the start that he would eschew what he called Yorkeological details. He went to the Doric order for a finite system of design and justified it on the grounds that 'the perfection of the order is far nearer Nature than

(Opposite)

Heathcote, Kings Road, Ilkley, Yorkshire: Edwin Lutyens (1906)

Heathcote is situated on one of the suburban terraces that rise above the town to the famed Ilkley Moor. It belongs to Lutyens' 'Georgian' period when he was at the height of his success, and anticipates the more formal, classical and pompous style of his public buildings phase. It is an exercise in Italiante; he would refer to it as 'Sanmichele'. Lutyens became deeply involved with the technical difficulties of using classical details – like coupling the columns and finding that the bases interlock. He

anything produced on impulse.' Like so many other architects of his time, he had discovered authority in Nature – but Nature properly studied and organized!

Lutyens was not finished with country houses after Heathcote for he went on to design over a hundred although that delightful and privileged world had been shattered by the Great War. For Lutyens, the War meant a major reorientation. It turned him in a direction which, but for the War, he might never have experienced but which was always inherent in his paradoxical personality. The classical architect lurking beneath the skin of the Arts and Crafts designer now came to the front and made a new contribution to the national scene.

At the beginning of July 1919 the Prime Minister, Lloyd George, sent for Lutyens and told him that the Government wanted a catafalque erected in Whitehall for the march past of allied troops in a fortnight's time. Lutyens sent in his design within a few days but because there were only ten days in which to build it, it was a temporary structure of wood and plaster. It was exactly what was wanted. It caught the imagination of the hundreds of thousands of people who passed it during the peace celebrations. It was so obviously right that it was rebuilt as a permanent structure. The sole inscription on it – 'To the Glorious Dead' – was suggested by Lloyd George. Its name, though, was suggested by

notes that Inigo Jones solved this problem, that Wren avoided it, that Vanbrugh failed lamentably. Lutyens succeeded. But it meant 'hard labour, hard thinking, over every line in all three dimensions and in every joint; and no stone can be allowed to slide.' Scrutiny of those details, however, reveal that he had been unable to resist introducing an English schoolboy jokiness. The pilasters on the front of the house do a Cheshire cat vanishing act, dying back into the wall to leave their classical smile only at top and bottom in the cap and the base. As always, the circulation space is ample and ingenious, areas highlit with contrasts of black and white in the marble of paving and staircases. This aspect of his genius can also be seen in the hall of Queen Mary's Dolls' House, and at Gledstone in Yorkshire, where the steps of the marble stair are (somewhat hazardously) alternately black and white.

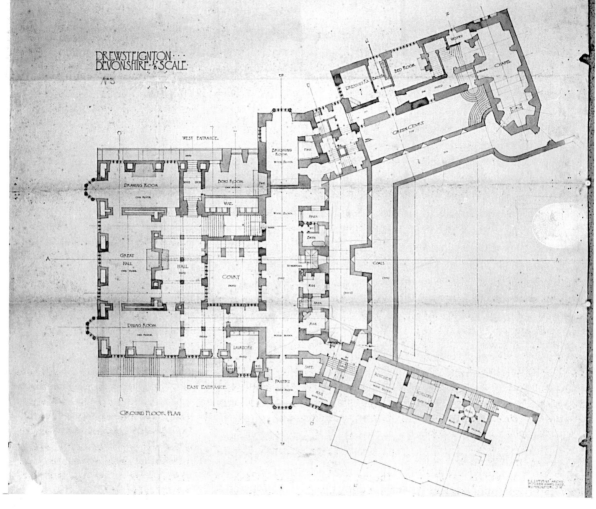

DREWSTEIGNTON
DEVONSHIRE · ½ SCALE·
Nº 5

GROUND FLOOR PLAN

(Opposite)

Castle Drogo, Drewsteignton, Devon: Edwin Lutyens (1910–30)

Lutyens was working on two castles at this period. But whereas Indian society still had a valid need for a Viceroy's House at New Delhi, Castle Drogo was an anachronism, for the First World War had destroyed in England the country house society which relied on plenty of servants and plenty of free time for shooting and week-end parties. Ten years earlier, the client of Grey Walls had insisted on a house when Lutyens wanted to try his hand at a Scottish castle. Now: 'I do wish he didn't want a castle, but just a delicious loveable little house with plenty of large rooms in it,' Lutyens wrote to Lady Emily of his client, Julius Drewe, the owner of the Home and Colonial Store chain. But what Drewe wanted was a granite castle on the edge of Exmoor, with a mediaeval hall and a tower, to cost £60,000. Eventually the scheme was cut by about two-thirds in the first ten years of building, and lost most of its south elevation. The massive walls, some 6 feet thick, rise sheerly to a castellated roofline, and vertical bands of fenestration are cut deeply back into the stonework.

Castle Drogo – plan:

The internal spaces flow, channelled by overhead vaulting into one another and from level to level. The service quarters are cut into the rock and each room is ingeniously lit. The walkways on the leads are particularly exciting. Unfortunately, the castle leaks badly.

(Above)

The Cenotaph, Whitehall, London: Edwin Lutyens

The Cenotaph (the name was chosen by Lutyens as meaning a tomb which does not contain the body it commemorates) figures to this day in the annual march past of November 11th, and has become a focal point world-wide for an expression of the grief and honour surrounding those who died in war.

Lutyens. Looking at a heavy garden seat years before, Miss Jekyll had remarked that it reminded her of the Cenotaph of Sigismunda. He looked up the meaning of cenotaph, which is: a tomb not containing the body of the person remembered. So it became The Cenotaph.

Its design is at first sight simple – an elegant coffin on top of a stylish plinth. That simplicity hides a professional sophistication which was a delicious exercise in architectural perfection for Lutyens. None of its lines are horizontal or vertical. If projected up into the sky, the verticals would meet at a point 1,000 feet above the monument; the horizontal lines have a shallow camber which is the curve of a circle with its centre 900 feet below the ground.

Lutyens was already working on war graves and monuments for the War Graves Commission. He was responsible for the great centrepiece of every cemetery – the stone of remembrance, the 'War Stone', erected in all Imperial War Graves Cemeteries and carrying simply the words 'Their Name Liveth for Evermore'. The verticals and horizontals had lines even more subtle than the Cenotaph.

Of all the monuments, one is arguably the finest piece of

Memorial at Thiepval, The Somme, France: Edwin Lutyens

Lutyens was one of the architects appointed to the War Graves Commission, whose task it was to sort out the graves on the battlefields of France. Disliking the religious divisiveness of a cross where not all soldiers of Empire or Commonwealth professed Christianity, he first devised the standard gravestone and then the 'War Stone' as the central feature of every graveyard – 'a great fair stone of fine proportions', 12 feet in length, set on three steps, every line of which was of subtly curved and calculated proportions. But the greatest monument he created was at Thiepval, at the top of a hill where a German Command Post once stood and on whose slopes poppies now blow in the corn. The monument is a complex of interlocking arches set at right angles to each other, in which every dimension and every proportion is mathematically exact; every component leads to the next component, the next stage in bigness or smallness on the same plane or at right angles. The entablature above the keystone over one arch turns the corner and becomes the springing line for the next arch. The interpenetrating spaces have the inevitability of death and the grandeur of grief; and at the same time expose 64 faces of Portland stone on which the names of those whose bodies were never recovered, who had been denied the dignity of burial, could be inscribed.

architecture he ever produced and possibly the greatest single work of the post-war years. That was the great arch at Thiepval in Belgium, the centrepiece of a huge cemetery for the fallen in the two Battles of the Somme, in July 1915 and March 1918. It had to record the names of the 73,357 soldiers missing at the Somme. Instead of inscribing them all on a wall, he seized the chance of creating a three-dimensional form with the maximum surface area so that all the names on that terrible list could be given dignified space. The complex of arches and planes that make the memorial, built of small reddish French bricks and Portland stone, is a masterpiece of dimensional coordination. It is also an extraordinary feat of imagination. One of his assistants once remarked of him that he could see in the round and he must indeed have done that at Thiepval. What was even more extra-ordinary was that such a precise exercise in mathematics could give shape to a structure of fantastic emotional power.

Lutyens' concern with mathematics was a means to realizing his obsession with modules and proportions. On the basis of experience he had established certain acceptable dimensions and angles. For example all inclined planes, such as roofs, should be at an angle of 54.45 degrees, which is the same angle as the diagonal of a classical window pane. He found the proportion of 1 to the square root of 2 satisfactory and used it widely. His favourite ratio of height to width was $2\frac{1}{2}$ times. His motto was *Metiendo Vivendum*. But, however magical a proportion, it does not explain the ability of the man to think in three dimensions, to have a three-dimensional vision. It's a very rare gift, as we have seen with Charles Rennie Mackintosh. Like him, Lutyens could not only see in the round; he could also see through solids as if they were transparent.

Lutyens became the most popular and successful British archi-tect of the inter-war years, designing banks, embassies, university buildings and, less successfully, housing. But it was his two great public buildings (one never to be finished) which gave him an especial status.

One of those commissions was considered the finest archi-tectural project undertaken by any English architect since Sir Christopher Wren. At the Coronation Durbar in 1911, King George V announced, to the delight of many and the utter consternation of some, that the capital of India was to be moved from Calcutta to Delhi and that a new capital city was to be built. The foundation stone was laid in 1911; the main buildings were opened with another Durbar and lavish celebration in 1931.

Lutyens was not the only architect involved since in addition to the Government architects, he brought in his old friend Herbert Baker to join him in the design of the overall plan. As far as the buildings were concerned, Baker was responsible for the Secretariats and the Assembly Building whereas Lutyens was responsible for the climax of the whole plan, the Viceroy's House. The disagreements of the two architects over the slope leading to the Viceroy's House have become one of the great quarrels in architectural history.

Whatever the merits of that argument, there has never been any doubt about the quality and grandeur of the Viceroy's House. It was a fitting home and palace for the ruler of the largest land in the British Empire. It was bigger than Versailles but much more compact. It was 650 feet by 530 feet and had 12 enclosed courtyards and 340 rooms. Everything was designed and supervized by Lutyens, partly in London and partly during his annual stays in Delhi, working on details. It was said to be the largest project ever undertaken by a single architect.

The Viceroy's House was grand both inside and out, in mass and in detail. The Mughal gardens are richly laid out and full of the imagination and fun that Luytens loved. He designed a fountain so that it would give a rainbow, and to his delight it worked. He also made a butterfly garden (which he had done in England ten years before) by planting in one area only those plants that attracted butterflies; close to it was a living and changing splash of colour.

Inside he was also responsible for the furnishings. Some antiques were imported from England, some crystal chandeliers were copied from old Indian houses; but everything else was his – the Viceroy's throne, the mantelpieces (all different), the fenders, fire-irons and fire-backs, the nursery chandeliers of painted wood with angels, horses, hens and chicks and broken eggshells spilling into light bulbs. The floor of the nursery was patterned in red and white so that you could play chess on it and in the centre of the nurseries was a wooden screen with a huge bird cage in each side. There was a small window to enable children to look down the main staircase at the guests.

Inside and out, Rathstrapati Bhavan (as it is now called), was a rich feast of joy and invention. Fusing East and West, Lutyens took the components of eastern architecture and developed them to meet the demands of the climate. For example, he took the wide lips of the domes and the screens that provide shelter from the sun and the fountains, that irrigate and cool the wide expanses, and submitted them to the remorseless logic of western classicism. There were stone umbrellas providing shade, elephants holding up the corners and a specially new Order, the Delhi Order, a kind of recessed capital, doing for the great palace what the Doric order had done for the Parthenon. There were also whimsical details such as the bells at the corner of the capitals. He had brought the whole place into one blazing, colourful unity. In the three or four hours it took to walk round the house there was a surprise for everyone and a richness of invention that made it a palace of

The Viceroy's House, New Delhi, India: Edwin Lutyens (1912–1931)

There is a saying that each time the rulers of India have built a new capital, the end of that era of rule is signified. In 1912, Lutyens was given the enormous commission to build a new capital for the largest land in the largest empire in the world. The new city was to be laid out to the south of the old city of Delhi with a vast two mile layout of government buildings and courts centred on a tree-lined avenue, the King's Way, that marches up Raisina Hill to the Viceroy's House at the top. Other architects collaborated. Lutyens was the architect for the Viceroy's House. 29,000 labourers were engaged in the great work which was eventually to give occupation to 6,000 servants. Today it houses the President of India. As one travels up the slope between the Secretariats, the smooth disc of the dome, echoing a Buddhist stupa, rises over the horizon, set on the long low plinth of the building itself. Colonnades for which Lutyens invented the new 'Delhi order' emphasize the horizontal calm and impeccable proportions. Lutyens used dull red and creamy-buff local sandstone, and set the Palace with its 340 rooms and 12 enclosed courtyards in beautiful Mogul gardens of the kind he had long admired.

delight. The 'schoolboy, artist and mystic' described by Lord Halifax when he was Viceroy had brought all three aspects together and made a huge new casket filled with treasures, personal and public, mysterious and grand.

The other great public building, and possibly Lutyens' greatest, was the one he never finished. Invited by the Catholic Archbishop of Liverpool to design a major cathedral for his diocese, Lutyens saw the project as an opportunity to express the unity of his belief in the ultimate with the capacity of architecture to reveal it. It was also an opportunity to put right previous architects' mistakes. Michelangelo's dome on St Peter's looked like a pimple, he thought, and was hidden from view by Maderna's façade. His own dome would be massively right, 509 feet from the floor to the top of the cross.

The whole cathedral was to have been on an outrageous scale, only a few feet shorter than St Peter's but far greater in volume, with twin aisles on each side of the nave, a vast crossing under the dome, and immense buttresses to support it, themselves threaded through with arches and spaces. There would be no buttresses obstructing the aisles as in Michelangelo's cathedral nor such a clumsy junction of arches and minor arches under the drum and dome as in Wren's St Paul's. There was to be an exact system of proportions. He used a repeated theme of one to three; there would be three circles to each bay and arch, the top one giving the shape of the arch, each bay 15 feet wide and 45 feet high.

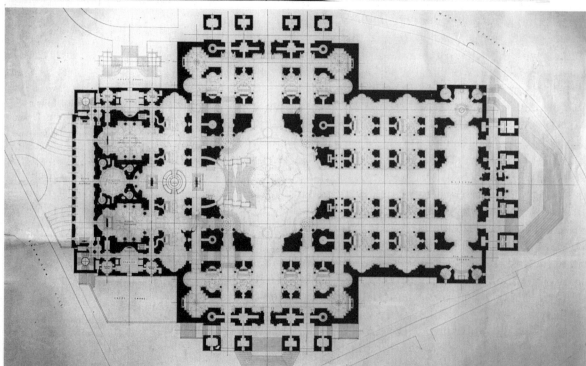

The plans and sections on which he spent the last years of his life are some of the most perfect examples of total three-dimensional thinking ever carried out on the drawing board by any architect in history. Every space, every corner, every gallery, every turning was considered and thought out. Every space has its axis and every axis is stopped and turned, either round or up or down. It is completely thought out three-dimensionally, with its axes and angles and levels. All of it can be read in the plan. Every space leads to another so that every movement is a sequence of spaces, each space has a before and after, a major and a minor.

Only the undercroft was built before work was stopped by the Second World War. After 1945, there were attempts to simplify the design to bring it within reasonable cost, but in the end the design was abandoned. It is difficult now to calculate what it would have cost. When they abandoned it in the late '50s it was thought that its completion would have required some £30 million – in today's prices, more than £500 million. It would have bankrupted any Church.

Lutyens left no school of imitators because by the time he died the architecture he represented seemed to be already at an end. He died with the plans for Liverpool Cathedral round him on the walls, surrounded by the perfect idea for the greatest building he had invented; there was already, as he lay there, no reason to build it and no possible financial resources for it. He had been the genius who created the modern English country house just in time for the cataclysm of the Great War which destroyed the very society that made such houses possible. He presided over the dying moments of three great architectural episodes – of country houses, of monuments and of palaces – and there was nothing to follow him. Lutyens had not wanted to join the history of his time, represented by the Modern Movement. The failure to do so, or the failure of the Modern Movement to recruit him, does not diminish Lutyens' achievements, nor does it make any comment upon the movement itself. What the Modern Movement tried to do was, after all, one of the great historical exercises in social idealism. Looked at with today's eyes it seems that it failed – and so Lutyens takes his place again as a major figure of his time.

He designed with knowledge, understanding and wit. The proportions of his buildings were impeccable; their plans the most original and ingenious ever known, derived from his inexhaustible study and observation of his clients' needs. It was a great tradition. He was, as his biographer wrote, 'the last great architect of the age of humanism'.

Liverpool Roman Catholic Cathedral: Edwin Lutyens (1933)

Started in 1933 on a nine acre site, it was calculated that this enormous project would take two centuries to complete. In fact, the Second World War stopped it and for reasons of finance it was never resumed. All that was completed, the crypt, now forms the foundations to Frederick Gibberd's cathedral, which occupies only a fraction of the space that Lutyens' cathedral would have taken up. To get an idea of the size, it may be helpful to note that one aisle of the undercroft which was built and houses the sacristy, could hold a thousand people at Mass. The whole building would have been flooded with light. He was convinced that light badly handled could destroy the architecture; his cathedral would throw light onto surfaces and define the spaces and shapes. The crypt was faced in granite, but he envisaged lots of black plaster surfaces on the vaults and domes which he felt suited the English climate.

Liverpool Cathedral – plan

Lutyens died with the plans and elevations on the walls around him. The plans and sections show as perfect an example of three dimensional thinking on the drawing board as any architect ever produced in history. The Archbishop's tomb in the crypt, closed with a rolling stone (a typical touch), is sited directly under where the high altar would have stood.

CHAPTER SEVEN

PROPORTION, MOVEMENT, SPACE & LIGHT

The Dominance of Le Corbusier

The work and ideas of Le Corbusier have to be discussed in any study of modern architecture; for knowledge of his work, for good or ill, is indispensable to the Modern Movement. His influence has been so colossal, so worldwide and so comprehensive that he dominates not only the world of architecture but, in effect, a great part of the world of invention and culture. He ranks with Darwin, Freud, Einstein, Wittgenstein and Picasso among major figures who have for ever affected the world to which we belong.

One of the recurrent ironies of history is that the end product of social ideology can be human misery. There can be no doubt that the ideology of Le Corbusier, or that of his many followers, in creating vast complexes of housing has been anything but successful in social terms and nowadays, their very image fills many people with horror. Le Corbusier played a key role in world-wide developments, as many of his contemporary architects have confirmed. His clarity, persistence and determination made it impossible to ignore him, even if it took some time for his message to be accepted.

In case there should be any danger of people not knowing about his work, Le Corbusier made sure that it was all, buildings and projects, realized and unrealized, published in regular volumes – the *Oeuvre Complete*, published in Zurich at regular intervals and then brought together in two omnibus volumes, the first covering 1910–1960 and the second 1910–1965. In addition, the volume written by Le Corbusier, *My Work* (1960), gave ample evidence of the fertility of his mind and the variety of his projects and ideas.

Charles Edouard Jeanneret (Le Corbusier) was a relatively late starter. The son of a watch engraver and a student of design, he was a painter, designer and writer before he created any of the buildings that made him famous. His studio and office in Paris were not set up until 1917 when he was already 40 years old. Its

Notre Dame Du Haut on Bourlemont Hill, Ronchamp: Le Corbusier (1950–5)

The pilgrimage chapel at Ronchamp was commissioned by the Diocesan Commission of Sacred Art of Besançon to replace a 19th-century church destroyed by artillery fire and paid for with a war indemnity grant. The post-war church rebuilding boom coincided with a revival of interest in the liturgy; Pere Couturier, editor of the influential *L'Art Sacré*, campaigned for the use of the best artists to achieve 'a sense of the sublime' and bring people back to the Church. The free brief – 'No programme other than the celebration of Mass, one of the oldest of human institutions ... (and a) pilgrimage place on specific days ...' – embraced a church with three side chapels, each expressed on the exterior with an apse, and emphasized by a tower which funnelled in the light, a presbytery, pilgrims' hostel and war memorial.

The fluid form of the design is no accident – the floor is marked with the dimensions of the Modulor, and the lines delineate the axes from which the shape is generated. He used brick and rubble from the old church, a reinforced concrete frame and a concrete roof supported on a series of point-supports incorporated into the wall frame to give a totally moulded exterior. The very thick south wall is slung beneath the roof – simply a reinforcement grid thickly sprayed with concrete from a cement gun through which light enters along irregularly positioned and angled shafts, to give a kinetic wall of living light and colour, changing as the day revolves.

growing reputation owed a lot to his cousin Pierre Jeanneret who, from all accounts, was a man of enormous charm and supreme competence in the organization of the projects for which the office became known all over the world.

What made Le Corbusier a compulsive figure was the series of articles about architecture published in the journal *l'Esprit Nouveau* and put together to make the book originally entitled *Vers une Architecture* (1923), translated as *Towards a New Architecture* and published in England in 1927. The change of title indicates a problem about Le Corbusier. *Vers une Architecture* or *Towards an Architecture* was exactly what he meant and he meant something enormous, universal, emotional, of world importance by the word *Architecture*. Similarly, a translation of his most notorious aphorism, 'a house is a machine for living in', does not communicate anything like the total meaning of *machine* as he meant it in French – a contrivance of huge significance and meaning under the control of man.

The impact of *Towards an Architecture* was devastating – wildly unpopular with established figures, a fantastic burst of light and revelation for many of the young.

'A great epoch has begun
There exists a new spirit'

he said at the start of every section. And it had the most devastating clarity. Not surprisingly, as the publisher's preface to the 1946 edition said in the first sentence, 'This book has probably had as great an influence on English architectural thought as any one publication of the last fifty years.'

As a measure of its lasting importance here are a few definitions from it:
– on *Mass*. 'Our eyes are constructed to enable us to see forms in light.'
– on *Surface*. 'A mass is enveloped in its surface, a surface which is divided up according to the directing and generating lines of the mass; and this gives mass its individuality.'
– on *Plan*. 'The plan is the generator. The plan holds within itself the essence of sensation.'
– on *Architecture*. 'The business of architecture is to establish emotional relationships by means of raw materials. Architecture goes beyond utilitarian needs. ... Passion can create drama out of inert stone.'
– on *The illusion of plans*. 'The Plan proceeds from within to without. The exterior is the result of the interior.'
'The elements of architecture are light and shade, walls and space.'
'Arrangement is the gradation of aims, the classification of intentions.'

Villa Les Terrasses/Stein de Monzie, 15 Rue de Pr. Pauchet Garches, Paris: Le Corbusier (1926–8)

This house is in the Parisian suburb of Vaucresson. Looking back on it at the end of his life, Le Corbusier called it the 'first phase of a manifested modern architecture'. In contrast to some earlier houses such as the Villa Fallet at La Chaux-de-Fonds which is colourful, cosy and strongly vernacular in its wide-eaved roof and Arts and Crafts woodwork on panelling and stairs, Garches establishes the classic pattern for an international modern house.

We can identify all Le Corbusier's five points: the reinforced concrete pilottis, a flat roof with roof terrace and solarium, a ribbon of sliding windows, a loose floor plan and free façade (which he had in earlier designs intended to be more formal with an ABABA rhythm). Accommodation comprised three main bedrooms, two guest, two servants' rooms and a lodge for the *gardien*, as well as public rooms and a spectacular series of terraces winding up to the roof garden. A running track was originally planned for the roof. Corbusier did not encourage a lazy and sybaritic life: he liked his clients to live the healthy life, persuading them into small and ascetic bedrooms and always providing steep stairs for exercise.

'Corb in his youth was Mr. Clean,
A house to him was just a machine,
And when his clients began to grouse,
He re-designed them to fit the house.'

So wrote Louis Hellman, sometime cartoonist to *The Architects' Journal*.

Le Corbusier goes on immediately to insist on the inevitability of mass-production houses:

'Industry on the grand scale must occupy itself with building and establish the elements of the house on a mass-production basis. We must create the mass production spirit –

The spirit of constructing mass-production houses
The spirit of living in mass-production houses
The spirit of conceiving mass-production houses.

'If we eliminate from our hearts and minds all dead concepts in regard to the house, and look at the question from a critical and objective point of view, we shall arrive at the "House-Machine", the mass-production house, healthy (and morally so too) and beautiful in the same way that the working tools and instruments which accompany our existence are beautiful.'

Resounding above and around all the other glowing statements is his central definition of architecture: 'Architecture is the masterly, correct and magnificent play of masses brought together in light.' In fact, the original French sentence does not say *masses* but *volumes*, which is more exact in view of Le Corbusier's insistence – like almost every other pioneer of modern architecture – that architecture starts with the interior. How the masses function comes in almost the next sentence: 'Our eyes are made to see forms in light: cubes, cones, spheres, cylinders, or pyramids are the great primary forms.'

Those are the classical solids. What made his vision of them modern and different was his dramatic conversion to the doctrine of Cubism. As a painter and the colleague of Cubist painters, he recognized that he could achieve in architecture more than he or they could ever do in painting – that is, see forms in movement. That is the key to understanding his buildings. He saw buildings as great cubes which he could divide inside into higher and lower spaces, as in the Pavilion de l'Esprit Nouveau of 1925, a composition that he used many times. The resulting abstract spaces could then be seen in movement.

Le Corbusier was, in his theories as well as his buildings, both a classical and a romantic. In the end he was a romantic. The classical side of him can be seen in his fundamental statements about houses, formulated to accompany the two houses he contributed to the Weissenhof exhibition in Stuttgart in 1927. 'We are dealing,' he said 'with architectural facts which call for an absolutely new way of building.' And he listed what he later called 'The Five Points of a New Architecture':

1   Columns of *pilotis*, to raise the building off the ground and let the garden continue through and under the building.
2   The *roof garden*, so that the land lost on the ground can be replaced up above. The key to that is concrete. The roof is to be

Villa Savoye, Poissy, near Paris: Le Corbusier (1928–31)

The villa is set in parkland and from the upstairs living rooms commands views of the rolling land to the west of Paris. Critics likened the house to a Palladian villa hovering like a spaceship. It is in fact a cement-rendered concrete block box set on concrete pilottis with a funnel shape upon the roof, and presents a smooth, perfected outline typical of Le Corbusier's Purist period. The pilottis are extremely slim and arranged in a well-spaced rectangular garland. Above floats the smooth box, sliced into three horizontally with a band of gleaming windows as the jam in the sandwich. As always, Le Corbusier's best architecture is for rich clients, and the spacious white hallways and palatial tiled bathroom with sunken bath are impressive.

of sand covered with thick cement slabs with staggered joints, the joints seeded with grass, terraces with flowers, shrubberies and trees, grass.

3 The *free plan*, made possible by the use of a few columns supporting slab floors (see the 'Dom-Ino House' diagrammatic model).

4 The *long window* round the whole house and free from the columns so that the house can be evenly lit.

5 The *free façade*. The exterior walls being no longer load bearing can be open or closed to suit the façade. They are now only light membranes composed of insulating or window elements.

With those points to go by he offers four compositions based on his own house designs for La Roche, Garches, Stuttgart, and the Villa Savoie. The villa, now designated as a building of historical importance, has been restored and is the most sophisticated example of his mature house designs.

What explains both the stature of Le Corbusier's thinking and later the unpopularity of his work is the fact that from the very start – explicitly in *Towards a New Architecture* – he conceived architecture and town planning as one. The house and the city revealed or were generated by the same principles. The mass-produced houses were the expression of a civic culture. Unlike Lloyd Wright, Le Corbusier was essentially a city man, endlessly excited by it. And the buildings he designed were ultimately components in the 'Radiant City' – his own phrase, indicating the character of the city of the future, which like the house would have light and space on top, lots of space between buildings, buildings on pilotis, gardens in the air on top.

All he now needed was a system of scale and proportion, to ensure that his buildings, free of traditional detail and composed of entirely new components, had a discipline of their own and a human scale appropriate for the new world of urban man. For the system of proportion he adapted the Golden Section (the brilliantly simple formula beloved by the architectural theorists and practitioners of the Renaissance), elaborated it and called it *Le Modulor*. That would establish a rational relationship between the parts of a building. But it was still necessary to give it a scale which would relate it not to a mathematical figure but, in true humanistic fashion, to man. To give the buildings a human scale he therefore took one of the numbers in the series and finding that it was not only a good basic module for a room but the regulation height for a London policeman, at that time the international symbol of law and order, sketched out the gesticulating diagram of a figure against the scale – Corbusian man.

The theory was complete. He spent the rest of his life implementing it. The most complete expression of those theories were the

Pavillon Suisse, Cité Universitaire, Paris: Le Corbusier (1931–3)

Although this job was carried out under 'the most difficult circumstances', Le Corbusier reckoned he had provided a 'laboratory' for modern architecture, particularly in the solution of technical problems over the dry stone walling and insulation between rooms achieved with inserting sheets of lead into the partition walls. The plan is T-shaped. The long-arm is formed by a slab block set on a single row of four concrete-encased steel stanchions; here are packed, on four storeys, the 51 student rooms. The short leg of the 'T' houses the refectory, gymnasium, library, etc. There is a curved staircase block attached, and a director's house and caretaker's lodge were also provided. The frescoes painted by Le Corbusier in 1948 stirred as much interest as did the architecture.

four huge housing schemes, the Unités d'Habitation de Grandeur Conforme at Marseilles, Nantes, Strasbourg and Berlin. I know two of them and have experienced the excitement that their builders and first inhabitants undoubtedly experienced, and some still do, despite what is often reported.

The most complete expression of the *Five Points* is, I think, in the few large houses built by Le Corbusier in India while designing and erecting the central massive buildings for the new capital of the Punjab, Chandigarh. The general plan was made by the English architects Maxwell Fry and Jane Drew. Le Corbusier was responsible for the capitol and its government buildings – the Secretariat, the Legislative Chamber, the Courts of Justice and the symbol of the hand. Massively constructed in concrete, they are a synthesis of his early experiments and pioneering buildings. The almost completely abstract Cubist design for the Shodan house at Ahmedabad is as complete a visual statement as he ever made

Unité Grandeur Conforme, Ave Michelet, Marseilles: Le Corbusier (1947–52)

Of his prefabricated housing units at Pessac in 1926, Le Corbusier had summarized his ideas thus: The aim – low cost; the means – reinforced concrete; the method – standardization, industrialization, tailorized mass production. During the war-years, in 1941, he had been appointed by the Vichy government to a committee to revitalize housing, but had been sacked after a few months. By the time this commission arrived from the French government, his purposes in building housing had become much more lyrical: 'First, to provide with silence and solitude before the sun, space and greenery, a dwelling which will be the perfect receptacle for the family; second: to set up in God's good nature, under the sky and sun, a magisterial work of architecture, the product of vigour, grandeur, nobility, happiness and elegance.' The Unité was a revolutionary concept: to house an entire community in one concrete slab block on stilts – a village in the air within a city. It has 18 storeys encompassing a selection of maisonettes to house families from childless couples up to those with five

children; a shopping street; social facilities such as a nursery and primary school, laundry, swimming pool and a hotel and restaurant. The housing units are slotted together on two levels front and back of the block, like a carpentry joint, to allow each house 1½ floor heights for varied arrangements of their units, and each has a double height living room. Once built, it has continued to provoke strong and ambivalent feelings from both occupants and critics. 'I think (says Philip Johnson) Marseilles must be one of the greatest buildings of all times ... if you don't go there too often. Under the pilottis is one hell of a place to be unless you want to pee.'

Governor's Palace, Chandigarh, Punjab, India: Le Corbusier (1950–85)

After the death of Matthew Novicki, the architect appointed to build a new capital city for the Punjab, a new contract was drawn up with Le Corbusier and his partner and cousin, Pierre Jeanneret. The site is at the foot of the Sivalik hills in the Himalayas, about 150 miles north of Delhi. The city layout was planned on a circulation grid by Maxwell Fry and Jane Drewe. Le Corbusier was ecstatic: 'It is the hour I have been waiting for ... India the humane and

profound civilization. ... To construct a capital: urbanism is the activity of a society. ... A Capital is the spirit of a nation. ...' The materials of city planning, he said, are 'sky, space, trees, steel, cement in that order and in that hierarchy.' There is not much said about people. Buildings include the Capitol complex of parliamentary, legal and administrative buildings (which includes the striking sculptured, open-sided box of the High Court), the Palace of Assembly and the Governor's Palace (not built). This last was designed to the Modulor, formed of square concrete interlocking boxes, the divisions expressing different functions – the halls of assembly, say, distinct from the guest rooms. Le Corbusier planned a garden of reflecting pools around it. On its roof is scooped out the umbrella shape with which Corbusier replaced the traditional Mhugal *chatris*, providing shade. People have associated this shape with Corbusier's obsession with bulls' horns, and also with the dignified form of a woman carrying a burden on her head which had so impressed him in India. This symbolic shape also appears on the upturned portico roof that runs along the side of the Parliament Building, supported on a series of great flanges that cast wedges of shade at intervals along the wall. But the theme is most explicit in the Monument of the Open Hand that rises above the open-air court of public assembly. Curved, palm upwards to the sky, fingers spread in a gesture often found on Buddhas, the Open Hand from one angle resembles a dove and symbolizes peace and reconciliation. Le Corbusier wanted to 'affirm that the second era of machinist civilization has begun; the era of harmony. ...' 'There is still time to choose, to equip ourselves rather than to arm. ...' At the Inauguration Ceremony in 1963, Nehru spoke of Chandigarh as 'a temple of the New India ... the first expression of our creative genius, flowering on our newly earned freedom.'

about the principles underlying the house as an examplar of modern architecture.

What still requires explanation as well as understanding is the legacy that Le Corbusier left in the field of housing. It cannot be too strongly emphasized that when the monumental complexes of housing went up, they were greeted with enthusiasm by critics as well as architects. It required two decades before critics of the social scene began to see his influence as malign, and the effect he had had upon the housing of many parts of the world as disastrous.

Two points have to be made about that change in esteem and Le Corbusier's influence upon architects of other countries. The first is that he was not responsible for what happened to the buildings of the copyists. For example, flat roofs. Le Corbusier's insistence upon flat roofs was not for economy or style; it was because in his view the ground lost by the building being put upon it should be regained on the roof. His roofs, therefore, became another place for living – not only a sun deck, as in some of the early houses, but a whole area for living and playing – on the Unité at Marseilles a playground, swimming pool and nursery school, at La Tourette a walkway, replacing the cloister of the traditional monastery.

The second point is, I believe, more fundamental. Le Corbusier was not really a social planner. He was an artist. He saw a social situation, a social problem – that of finding dwellings for large numbers of people in an egalitarian society – and literally visualized a solution. In other words, he did not follow a line of quantitative reasoning; he imagined an instant solution. And it was a vision that captured the imagination not only of himself and his colleagues but of the politicians and the potential tenants.

By saying that, I do not mean that he was irrational. Far from it.

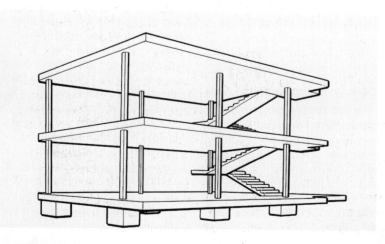

Diagram of the Dom-Ino House: Le Corbusier (1914–15)

Le Corbusier's basic house-building kit, evolved with Max Dubois. Six steel supports hold up rectangular slabs of concrete, cantilevered over the edges. A stairway zig-zags between levels. This kit, economical and easily prefabricated, allowed free-flowing of both plan and wall façades, since these are independent of the structure. A diagram fundamental to modern architecture.

He was using the faculty of direct perception rather than discursive reasoning. And he used it continuously. He used the discoveries of every building he created in the next building – the spatial arrangement of the Esprit Nouveau comes up time and time again. The windows, the undulating wall, all become part of his vocabulary, improved with use and used again. By the end, he had a complete dictionary of components, all thought out by him and developed by the team in his office.

But what they all have in common is that he saw them as an artist sees his creations. He saw a simple building for an exhibition as a work of art. He saw a simple house as a work of art. He saw a great housing complex – a Unité – as a work of art. He saw the whole city as a work of art and called it the Radiant City. He saw a whole region, like North Africa, as a work of art and he saw a new city like Chandigarh as a work of art, giving everyone the impression that he was the artist who had created it, even though he only handled the Government centre. That was a work of art quite big enough.

What happened to Le Corbusier was, in effect, not unlike what happened to Gaudi. What started as an original idea was enlarged to the point of absurdity. A vision of a pavilion or a house could embrace a hostel, a club, a residence. Once it reached the scale of a complex of housing it was dangerous but on the scale of a city it was fantasy – dangerous fantasy, a demonic vision of a kind to which architects seem often to be prone. It led to tragedy: social

Maison Jaoul, 81 bis Route de Longchamp, Neuilly-sur-Seine, Paris: Le Corbusier (1951–5)

Two houses, A and B, set at right angles on a narrow site, have similar plans with living rooms and library on the ground floor (the Jaoul parents' house also has a chapel), three to four bedrooms on the first floor and one to two bedrooms on the top floor. As befits a week-end house, it is deliberately rough outside. Le Corbusier used rough brick with heavy concrete lintels and concrete vaults made by pouring light concrete over Catalan brick vaults based on Gaudi's vaults of which Corbusier cherished a memory from a visit to Barcelona in 1928. Sunk in foliage and insulated with grass on the roof, the houses present the external appearance of romantic bunkers. Inside, the brick-faced vaults and tiling all have a smooth, high-class affluent finish – very beautiful.

ideas that were only really visual ideas became destructive of human happiness.

The mania did not, however, lessen Le Corbusier's ability to imagine wonderful new artefacts. As the great megalomaniac structures were rising in France and India and Germany, towards the end of his life he created two buildings which brought together all his discoveries and resulted in what is often considered the finest of all buildings in the Modern Movement – La Tourette and the chapel at Ronchamp.

The Dominican monastery of La Tourette at Eveux was built just in time for the Dominican Order to go through a major internal crisis related to the Second Vatican Council. Thus, it became obsolete within a few years of its arrival – all the more tragic in that it precisely satisfied the brief and was tailor-made as the study house for the Order of Preachers in France.

Now inhabited by a few friars and used (successfully) as a centre for conferences, La Tourette is a textbook of modern architectural components. It was built in 1957/60 and had a relatively simple programme. It was to be the study house for the Dominican Order, with cells or rooms for up to a hundred teachers and students, study halls and recreation room, a library and a refectory as well as the chapel.

On a steeply sloping site, Le Corbusier banked the two floors of cells above the community rooms and set the whole structure on concrete piles. The rooms are acoustically isolated, their concrete frames forming loggias and balconies. The windows of the communal rooms use the 'undulating wall', that is, a spacing of concrete mullions dictated by musical intervals in an undulating melody. The windows of the reception rooms express the different functions of a window.

The cloisters are in two sections: a straight section leading to the refectory, and a more continuous one on the roof. That, as well as the roof of the side chapels, is planted with grass, surrounding concrete roof lights, 'canons of light', illuminating the chapels below. The roof has thus once again recaptured the ground lost by building. The monastery was a demonstration of one of the fundamental precepts of the Modern Movement – that the functions of a building should be drastically reviewed and re-examined so as to form a new totality wholly of its own time.

But the supreme example of his command of architectural form and the exercise of his creative powers, seen through form and structure and light, was the Pilgrimage Chapel of Notre Dame du Haut at Ronchamp, near Belfort, built between 1950 and 1954. It lies on the last spur of the Vosges, above the plain of the river Saone. The former pilgrimage chapel dedicated to the Blessed Virgin and housing a reputedly miraculous statue was destroyed during the 1939–45 war.

Monastery of Ste Marie de la Tourette, Eveux-sur-Arbresle near Lyons: Le Corbusier (1953–9)

The client for this monastery and seminary to include cells, church, library and teaching rooms, was the Lyons Chapter of the Dominican order. It is now a conference centre. Le Corbusier saw the monastic life as a microcosm of society: the concern with space and austerity he had built into the Unités were clearly the basic considerations here. The plan was for concrete boxes set on thick pilottis ranged round an open quadrangle. Originally, the cloisters were to be round the grass-covered roofs, but this was altered to a cross-shaped cloister within the quadrangle, bridging from one side to another of the building. There were difficulties about the changes of level, and a 9 per cent incline makes the cloisters less than satisfactory. The friars' cells are shown in a double row of windows on the top floor; the famous 'undulating wall' of windows runs along the first floor level of the public rooms; internal corridors are long and high and meanly lit from above and somewhat claustrophobic. The church is lofty and plain. The distinctive bell-tower is a Cubist exercise, the projecting box-shape which holds the bell being mirrored right down the bland wall below by the box-shapes of the shuttering patterns on the concrete.

The new chapel had to hold only a few people inside (a congregation of 200 is possible only if most are standing) but provide for as many as 10,000 outside. The chapel must therefore express the meaning of the outside space as much as the interior. It does so by making all the forms curve outwardly and end only with the horizons – the boundary of the site is thus formed by the hills on the far side of the plain.

Le Corbusier wrote that he had the inspiration for the roof by looking at the shell of a crab picked up on Long Island and lying on his drawing board. The roof sags down in the middle and is composed of two membranes of concrete more than two metres apart. It does not touch the walls but rests on short struts leaving a crack of light between the walls and roof; it 'will amaze', said the architect. And the most dramatic wall, the south wall, slopes and contracts as it rises; it is 3.7 metres at the base and slims to 1.4 metres at the top.

He insisted that the curved volumes were derived from rectilinear generators. The floor is marked with the dimensions of *Le Modulor* and the lines delineate the axes from which the shape is generated. Le Corbusier described the chapel as 'an acoustical statement in the realm of form' and wrote: 'An implacable mathematics and physics reign over the forms presented to the eye. Their agreement, their repetition, their interdependence, and the spirit of unity or family which binds them together to form an architectural expression, is a phenomenon which is as supple, subtle, exact and implacable as that of acoustics.'

In the early houses, influenced by Cubist theories, the spaces were to be seen in movement. Now, at Ronchamp, the spaces would themselves be moving as the sun moved round and the light changed – the chapel is a study in mass and light illustrating many years after he first announced it, Le Corbusier's declaration that architecture is the masterly, correct and magnificent play of mass brought together in light. And the light is used to create the life of a constantly changing building. The miraculous statue is placed in a revolving window above and to the right of the altar and the glare of the light increases its mystery. Small square windows are cut through the east wall at different angles so that they lighten and darken differently during the day. The great sloping south wall, too, is a masterpiece of modularly spaced openings, with huge splays and openings filled with glass which Le Corbusier describes as *vitrages* rather than *vitrail*, not a picture but part of the architecture. The interior of one of the side chapels is bright red.

The interior components are carefully placed to express a theme. The great cross is not on the axis behind the altar but to one side where it becomes the Witness, the Tree, embedded in the ground. So the protagonists (as Le Corbusier saw them) became apparent; the Sign of the Cross on the axis of the altar, the Tree as witness and the Miraculous Statue – the presence of the Virgin Mary to whom the chapel is dedicated. With the chapel at Ronchamp, Le Corbusier came as close as he possibly could to his idea of *l'éspace indicible* – the miracle of inexpressible space, which in his view was what architecture ultimately has to aspire to.

In his writing, as well as his painting and architecture, Le Corbusier was far from being the bloodless rationalist he has sometimes been mistaken for. Almost as if he was echoing Lloyd Wright or Gaudi, he wrote in a letter to young architects in 1936:

'How are we to enrich our creative powers? Not by subscribing to architectural reviews, but by undertaking voyages of discovery into the inexhaustible domain of Nature! . . . I wish that architects would sometimes take up their pencils to draw a plant or a leaf – or to express the significance of the clouds, the ever-changing ebb and flow of waves at play upon the sands . . .'

CHAPTER EIGHT

FUNCTION AND ANONYMITY

The International Style

The figure of Le Corbusier towers over the Modern Movement as its presiding genius – artist, writer, architect, town planner, more influential than any other architect in the 20th century. In the last chapter we saw his work as an artist and architect and isolated some of the unquestionably great buildings that came from his studio. Now we must see it in another dimension. His influence upon the wider field of housing and town planning was for a time even more profound – and, I think, even more disastrous.

It was one of the most influential characteristics of the Modern Movement that for the first – and, in view of what happened, probably the last – time in the history of architecture, the housing of the ordinary man and woman became the material from which, it was thought, a great architecture could be generated. Architecture could be a definitive component in the social revolution; and because that involved the housing of many people – for every man and every woman – it had to be a key component in the organization of towns. As the building of houses is the bulk of all building it was argued that housing and town planning must be one. To the modern architect, town planning became an obsession.

But it was not the town planning seen in the Garden Cities or the suburbs of the turn of the century. Like the town plans of the mediaeval and Renaissance cities, that was on a relatively small scale – a human scale, in which it was possible to visualize the homes of families and individuals and cater for great variety in a humane landscape. Instead, the social revolution required planning on an altogether bigger scale, a scale on which statistics rather than descriptions become the basis of planning – the statistics of a social ideology rather than an individual human need. If only the two could be brought together, a great new city or town might be brought into being; all that was needed was a general rule for a universal solution.

In that development, Le Corbusier played a major part through the organization which brought together the theorists and practitioners, the *Congrès Internationaux d'Architecture Moderne* (CIAM), founded in 1928. Its influence was definitive and lasted (with interruptions) until 1956 when it broke into two and was succeeded by one part, Team X, and finally dissolved in 1959. In two periods, 1930–4 and 1950–5, it was, in the words of the historian Reyner Banham, the major instrument through which the ideas of modern architecture were made known to the world. The manifestos of the La Sarraz Declaration of 1928 and the Athens Charter of 1933, signed at the end of a great voyage of argument through the Mediterranean, shook the architectural world. Containing no less than 111 propositions, the 1933 Charter produced the definition of the five headings under which all town planning studies should be made – Dwellings, Recreation, Work, Transportation, and Historic Buildings. With somewhat less emphasis upon the last category, those categories were to shape the plans of several decades.

The Athens Charter not only defined the categories, it also declared that there should be a rigid functional zoning of city plans, with green belts between the areas reserved for the different functions. And there should be a single type of urban housing, with 'high widely spaced apartment blocks wherever the necessity of housing high densities of populations exists'. The effect of that policy upon the cities of Europe and America can be only too readily seen. For Le Corbusier it resulted in the great Unités d'Habitation of Marseilles and Nantes, Strasbourg and Berlin.

At the same time, there was a corresponding development in smaller scale architecture inspired by the same ideas but resulting in even more impersonal buildings. The CIAM Declaration of 1928 had insisted that, 'It is only from the present that our architectural work should be derived'. To achieve it, there must be a 'harmony of existing elements – a harmony indispensable to the present – by putting architecture back on its real plane, the economic and social plane; therefore architecture should be freed of the sterile influence of the Academies and of antiquated formulas'. How should that be done? The answer was clear and simple – 'the most efficacious production is derived from rationalisation and standardisation'.

It seemed that a new mass culture – of production, consumption and communication – was attainable, reflecting the new social orders emerging in the socialist and fascist states. So, architecture was seen to be (as it had occasionally before), not just a reflection of, but a definitive agency in, the creation of a new society. That

The Bauhaus at Dessau: Walter Gropius (1925)

The Dessau Bauhaus has been spoken of as 'Gropius's architectural manifesto, a visible expression of all the Bauhaus stood for.' Gropius in his school of art at Weimar in 1919, in a mood of post-war euphoric idealism, had planned to train architects and designers for the 20th century, uniting the world of art and the world of work. 'Let us create the new building of the future, which will embrace architecture *and* sculpture *and* painting in one unity and which will one day rise toward heaven from the hands of a million workers like the crystal symbol of a new faith.' On April 1st, 1925 the Bauhaus moved from Weimar to Dessau, where the Town Council commissioned from Gropius a group of buildings to include students' quarters, lecture rooms and workshops. 'For their construction and equipment, I brought the whole body of teachers and students into active co-operation. The acid test of attempting to co-ordinate several branches of design in the actual course of building proved entirely successful ... the band of fellow workers inspired by a common will I had once dreamed of now became a reality. ...' The upper floors of the workshop wing are cantilevered out and completely clothed in a skin of glass on a metal grid, the work and workers inside clearly exposed. The students' hostels have bands of windows cut across by projecting square balconies with tubular railings. 'The wholeness of (our) approach has helped to restore the architecture and design of today as a social art,' said Gropius. Another member, Paul Klee said 'We began over there in the Bauhaus. We began with a community to which each of us gave what he had. More we cannot do.' The Bauhaus closed in 1933.

society was of course to be international; the new architecture would therefore be international too.

The term 'International Style' was coined in 1932 by the organizers of the first International Exhibition of Modern Architecture, at the Museum of Modern Art in New York. The book produced for the exhibition declared that 'there is now a single body of discipline, fixed enough to integrate contemporary style as a reality and yet elastic enough to permit individual interpretation and to encourage natural growth.'

The latter part of the statement might be disputed but what was profoundly and widely influential was the nature of that single body of discipline. In the words of the organizers: 'There is, first, a new conception of architecture as volume rather than mass. Secondly, regularity rather than axial symmetry serves as the chief means of ordering design.' The new architecture would, in short, be designed from the inside and would be rectilinear. Only one more rule was necessary. To complete the prescription for a genuinely international approach, unsmirched by irrational or local characteristics, ornament was condemned.

If the insistence upon simplicity, regularity and volume rather than mass indicates the most obvious features of the International Style, it was a much more deeply felt concern for the kind of spaces that would characterize the style that inspired the leading architects on the Continent and America. That was the influence of Cubism. Launched by painters and then designers in the early years of the century, the dominance of the Cubist vision meant that, as in many other periods of architectural development, it was the artists who created the most lasting elements in the Modern Movement.

It is difficult to exaggerate the excitement felt by the artists who recognized the power of a new dimension. If Gaudi had discovered the magic of natural form and structures; if Wright had discovered the unity created by the continuity of inside and outside and the use of interpenetrating forms; and if Mackintosh had recognized the poetry of simple elements in three dimensions, it was the Cubist painters who discovered a still further dimension in interpenetrating space. That was the *fourth* dimension – of space seen in time.

The artists of the Renaissance might have been obsessed with the magic of perspective and the geometry enabling them to create precise spaces. Now scientists had found that in terrestrial terms space could only be described from more than one point of reference. Space is understood from a moving point of reference, the basis of the theory of Relativity. For artists it was a moment of revelation. An object could become more real if it was seen from more than one viewpoint – if possible, more than one at the same time. While that could be attempted in a painting, in architecture

it meant something both simpler and more effective. Buildings were now designed to be seen by an observer in movement rather than by a static observer such as was assumed in classical compositions. And since both the observer and users of a building could be assumed to be in movement in any case, here was something more real and positive than ever before – a simple but profound recognition of a truth.

Having therefore thrown off the tyranny of the historic styles and discarded their dead ornament, what would compose the architecture? Lines and planes and volumes. The planes of a building, like the planes of a cubist painting, would be the basic components of the architecture. And colour would also be a plane – clear primary colours like blue and yellow and red, held in place by simple whites, greys and blacks. They would reveal the 'new conception of architecture, as volume rather than mass'.

All that was now needed was the organization that would spread the word internationally with authority and vigour. It happened in the form of a school, the Bauhaus, founded by Walter Gropius in 1919. It moved to Dessau in 1925 but the changing political forces in Germany at that time forced the closure of the school in 1933 when its leading teachers left for the United States to escape the Nazi regime. Their move had a lasting effect upon architecture as it ensured that the Bauhaus message spread across the world.

The School taught design, building and craftsmanship. Under Gropius' direction (and assisted by brilliant artists such as Paul Klee, Wassily Kandinsky and Laszlo Moholy-Nagy), it insisted on

Housing in The Siemensstadt Siedlung, Berlin: Walter Gropius (1929)

In the Siemensstadt housing, Gropius combined 19th-century idealism with 20th-century realism. 'A breach has been made with the past, which allows us to envisage a new aspect of architecture corresponding to the technical civilization of the age we live in ... we are returning to honesty of thought and feeling. ...' The Siemensstadt flats were to prove a model for housing in a new age. Small (calculated at $2\frac{1}{2}$ to $3\frac{1}{2}$ rooms per flat) they were arranged in long white blocks, five storeys in height, and set among grass and trees. Two flats opened off each landing, and all were carefully orientated to gain maximum sunlight through large windows.

the fundamental unity underlying all branches of design and emphasized the necessity for a rational and systematic analysis as the start of any serious programme of building. The buildings of the Bauhaus, designed by Gropius, were a demonstration of these principles and those of the International Style too – simple elemental shapes, arranged according to their function, seen in movement as changing sequences of solid and transparent. The theory, teaching and form of the buildings became known world-wide.

One of the Bauhaus teachers, Mies van der Rohe, designed the housing for the Weissenhofsiedlung at Stuttgart in 1927. With its flat roofs and terraces, the scheme has had a lasting effect upon the design of domestic architecture. The most complete and expressive of all individual houses, however, was in the Netherlands – the Schroeder House by Gerrit Rietveld (1923–4). An impeccable Cubist construction of smooth planes set at right angles and articulated by bright primary colours, the interior walls can be slid away to make a large uninterrupted space. Here was indeed regularity rather than symmetry, volume rather than mass. As in

Factory for the Werkbund Exhibition, Cologne: Walter Gropius and Adolf Meyer (1914)

As in their factory for Fagus at Alfeld-an-der-Leine of 1911, the structure is fully exposed, the walls interpreted as a glass and steel membrane barely interrupted by structural piers, and the windows wrapping themselves round the corners to add to the transparent effect. It was an unprecedented use of glass and steel. Gropius believed he owed much to Peter Behrens, whose office he joined in 1907 (a staff later to be joined by Mies van der Rohe and still later by Le Corbusier). 'When I embarked on my career as an architect, the prevalent concept of architecture ... was dominated by

'one of the best buildings of its date in England, if not the best.' He goes on: ... 'the pattern for much to come (including most of the progressive schools built after the Second World War), in so far as at Impington the practical and visual advantages of modern forms in a loose yet coherent, completely free-looking arrangement has been demonstrated. Can it have been the effect of English picturesque notions on the more rigid intellect of Gropius?' There is bright colour in the red-brick buttress walls with yellow facings, in blue tiles and brightly painted ironwork. New ground was broken for classroom design with walls made of windows to ground level – a feature now heavily critizied by educationists. The County Architects Department has since made additions.

German Pavilion at Barcelona Exhibition: Mies van der Rohe (1929)

This temporary exhibition structure to display contemporary German culture established Mies's reputation. The low, tent-like structure on a travertine podium reflected in two pools is so understated it withdraws into a well-bred, silent and immaculate presence. It cannot be ignored, but speechlessly puts to shame other gaudier efforts, like a highly-sophisticated, well-groomed woman at a party. Structurally it is a one storey, dom-ino frame with a slab roof. Mies himself said of it: 'It is very important for our culture and our society, as well as for technology and industry, to find good solutions. German industry, and, indeed, European industry as a whole, must understand and solve these specific tasks. The path must lead from quantity to quality, from the extensive to the intensive. ... Along this path industry and technology will join with the forces of thought and culture.'

the classical orders. ... It was Peter Behrens who first introduced me to logical and systematic co-ordination of the handling of architectural problems ... I became obsessed by the conviction that modern constructional technique could not be denied expression in architecture, and that that expression demanded the use of unprecedented forms.'

Impington Village College, Cambridgeshire: Walter Gropius and Maxwell Fry (1936)

The rural community and education centres known as village colleges were the brain child of Henry Morris who, says his biographer Harry Rée, is 'the begetter of the Community School. He invented and created the Village College. He introduced the New Architecture to school building, and put colour and original art into the classroom.' Since Impington was thus a meeting of ideals in social justice, education and architecture, Gropius was the ideal architect for the job. He made six designs for Cambridgeshire County Council, the scheme constantly pruned, until Morris began to fear that 'one of the most significant advances in State education in the post-war period' would founder for lack of funds. However, the final complex of classrooms (for both adults and schoolchildren), clinics, libraries and social institutes planned in wings spreading out from a central concourse, won Pevsner's praise as

(Above)

Tugendhat House, Brno, Czechoslovakia: Mies van der Rohe (1930) (now destroyed)

The house is entered off the street at the higher level, a somewhat unpromising approach. Inside, spaces are set free to roam, with an entire wall of glass to the garden, and a terrace included in the plan. The public living areas are divided from each other only by screens, notably a semi-circular screen of macassar ebony round the dining area.

Schroeder House, Utrecht:
Gerrit Rietveld (1923–4)

Rietveld, an admirer of Berlage,
joined the De Stijl movement of
artists 12 years after its foundation
in Leiden in 1917. This house shows
the working out of Cubist planes
favoured by the Group with the
highly three-dimensional
manipulation of space Rietveld shows
in his own designs for chairs, with
their square members and unbent
plywood 'visibly connected' (as he
said). The owner collaborated with
him on the design of the cut-space
interlocking rooms, whose first floor
uses sliding panels in the Japanese
manner to separate sleeping, living
and working areas.

(Opposite, below)

Crown Building, Illinois
Institute of Technology,
Chicago: Mies van der Rohe
(1940–52)

most other countries, the inspiration for the architecture came
from painting. Piet Mondrian, one of the founders of the movement in Holland known as De Stijl, used interlocking geometric
forms, smooth bare surfaces and primary colours in his paintings
and constructions. A concise expression of the De Stijl principles
can also be seen in W. M. Dudok's new Town Hall (1928–30) at
Hilversum.

In England, the most celebrated examples of the International
Style were the houses by Amyas Connell (who had studied at the
British School in Rome and learned there about the work of Le
Corbusier) and Maxwell Fry, who worked with Gropius on the
latter's way from Germany to America during the '30s. The most
dramatic impact was made by another *émigré*, this time from
Russia, Berthold Lubetkin. His Penguin Pool at London Zoo was a
spiral of concrete descending into the water. The firm he founded,
Tecton, created at Highgate, London the most accomplished
example of the International Style seen in Britain. That was
Highpoint. It was a logical step from that to the post-war work of
the London County Council in housing and that of the Ministry of
Education in schools.

At the end of the war, the Architects Department of the London

'I believe that architecture has little
or nothing to do with the invention
of interesting forms or with personal
inclinations. True architecture is
always objective, and the expression
of the inner structure of our time
from which it springs.' Yet in this
group of regular, steel-framed boxes
with their smooth infill of brick or
glass, Mies van der Rohe was forced
to cover the steel frame he wanted to
express in a layer of fireproof
material, dishonestly retrieving
'honesty' by delineating the structure
in steel on top of the cladding – a
subterfuge commonly adopted on
would-be 'honest' structures today,
as in the Exhibition Hall at La
Valette, Paris. However, the Crown
Hall, the architecture school for the
Illinois Institute of Technology,
blatantly suspends its roof from
girders held up by steel columns, so
leaving a spacey and uncluttered
interior.

(Opposite, above)

Hilversum Town Hall, Hilversum, Holland: Willem M. Dudok (1928–30)

Dudok trained as a military engineer and was a member of the De Stijl group. He blended the conservative with the radical at Hilversum to create a deceptively simple and authoritative building that has full dignity but is not pompous. One-storey wings stretch out from a square courtyard, with a tall clock tower on one corner. Most of the main offices are on the ground floor, with the public rooms above. Outside, he employed buff-coloured brick in the fine Dutch tradition of brick building. Inside, the spaces and colours are finely chosen and immensely restful.

(Opposite, below)

Penguin Pool, London Zoo, Regents Park, London: Berthold Lubetkin/Tecton (1933–4)

Lubetkin was born in Russia, studied in Paris with Perret, and was imbued with the social idealism of the Soviet Revolution (he designed the Soviet Pavilion for Strasbourg in 1929) and of Le Corbusier's 'five points of a new architecture'. He formed the Tecton partnership in London with six Englishmen in 1930, and, with Ove Arup as engineering advisor, they designed the Gorilla House and the strikingly original Penguin Pool for London Zoo. To encourage the penguins' natural propensity to show off in queues and so delight the children (though in fact rendered screen walls block small children's view), two interlacing spirals of heavily steel-reinforced concrete curve upwards to provide parade ground and diving board over a shallow pool. Pillars, ledges and apertures encourage fun, and surfaces in concrete, slate and rubber provide variety for penguin feet.

Highpoint Flats, Highgate, London: Lubetkin & Tecton (I: 1933–5, II: 1938)

The Architectural Review of January, 1936 speaks of Highpoint I as 'one of the two or three examples in modern England ... that can be judged by international standards'. Tall, clean-lined and very expensively finished in reinforced concrete, the eight-storey flats on pilottis have a cross of Lorraine plan and stand on a green site commanding views over London. True to Le Corbusier's 'five points' the flats share a common ground floor and a public roof terrace. But they are not built on the dom-ino principle: the walls are load-bearing.

County Council had recruited several teams of young architects, some of them returning from military service, most with reasonably balanced left-wing views and all with ebullient post-war social idealism. In the '50s they produced some of the purest and most competent expressions of the International Style seen anywhere in the world. Of the major individual buildings, the best was the Royal Festival Hall, designed and developed at staggering speed in time for the Festival of Britain in 1951 by a team of architects, engineers and specialists under Robert Matthew, Architect to the Council. The Festival Hall brought together the modern understanding of space, a distinctively British approach to applied decoration and, probably for the first time, a systematic, rational study of needs, of circulation and above all of the acoustics demanded of a great space for orchestral concerts. Subsequent alterations robbed it of some of its character but the main achievement remains – possibly the best example of Gropius' demand for a systematic approach to the solution of architectural problems.

The same office also took over housing and was responsible for its own version of the mass housing being erected in many countries after the War. In Britain, this style was called mixed development, combining as it did, 11-storey slab and point blocks, four-storey maisonettes and two and one-storey houses in open

Royal Festival Hall, South Bank, London: London County Council Architects Department (1951)

Peacetime brought the International Style to Britain with fireworks in the Festival of Britain. The first public building to use the style was the Festival centrepiece – the Festival Hall – designed by London County Council Architects Department with Leslie Martin, Peter Moro and Edwin Williams under the leadership of Robert Matthew. Light sheath walls and internal partitions are supported on a frame of reinforced concrete pillars. The front has been changed from Matthew's patternwork of large and small windows which he thought imparted 'a jolly atmosphere' and is now much duller. The auditorium holds 2,600 seats. It was conceived as a box within the outer box of the building, releasing the space underneath the auditorium for circulation and social spaces. The

landscaped gardens. The most celebrated (and still attractive despite the later unpopularity of mass high housing) is the housing at Roehampton in London.

Even more socially conscious, and ultimately more successful in bringing together designers, researchers and clients (in the form of teachers and children as well as inspectors and administrators), was the school building programme in Britain. Enlarging on experiments made before the War, the ideology of that programme combined the fundamental conviction that the new architecture must be for everyone, of all classes and all interests, and it was determined to use industrial discoveries and techniques to produce suitable schools. In Hertfordshire and then in Nottinghamshire and other counties influenced by the recommendations of the architects of the Ministry of Education, the new schools were not simply light and airy structures in green fields; they were the calculated result of collaboration between users and designers, working to a performance specification agreed between them. They fulfilled the basic requirement of modern architecture as understood at the time – without historical styles, plain and anonymous, modular and practical.

'box' theme is repeated in the boxes of the concert hall which have an amusing resemblance to a chest of drawers with all the drawers pulled out. The colours are dark and warm – rich wood colours and leather in black and reds. The Hall became the model for a new breed of concert halls, due particularly to innovation in two areas. First, it introduced a sequence of flowing interior spaces, characteristic of the Modern Movement, particularly noteworthy in the circulation and social areas of the foyers and in the generously sweeping cantilevered staircases. Second, it was the first building to demonstrate comprehensively the application of the new acoustics; sound had to be controlled not only inside the hall, but also kept outside, since the Hungerford railway bridge runs directly alongside the Hall.

Flats at Roehampton: London County Council Architects Department, Chief Architect Robert Matthew

One of the first groups of high-rise housing in London. The London County Council Architects Department retained mature trees in the undulating parkland and between them built what came to be known as 'mixed development' – 11 storey slab and point blocks mixed with single storey, two and four storey blocks to house the old and families with small children. It was a characteristically British modification of Le Corbusier's theories, fused with lessons learnt from Scandinavia. Now that the inadequacies of high-rise housing have been demonstrated, the estate looks less attractive; in its day it seemed a heroic image of a post-war society housed on a massive scale.

The most complete expression of the movement, especially the policy of using prefabricated systems of building of which the most sophisticated was that developed by a Consortium of Local Authorities – CLASP – was the new University of York. With quietly restrained CLASP colleges loosely grouped around a new 18-acre lake, the 200-acre site was richly landscaped as a central part of the total concept. The prefabricated system resulted in speed of construction and the landscaping made for the agreeably humane social environment hoped for by the believers in a social architecture.

While York University may be recognized historically as the main British triumph of the International Style, it was in the United States that the movement found its fullest expresion and ultimately its demise. Another *émigré*, the Austrian Richard Neutra, produced an impeccable example with the Health House in Los Angeles, designed for the healthy life enthusiast Dr Philip Lovell. Built in 1927–9, it is a predominantly white, airy house looking out over a romantic landscape, created from a steel frame with a lightweight synthetic skin as well as glass. After the War, in 1946–7, Neutra produced an even more sophisticated and elegant statement with the Kaufmann House at Palm Springs.

Of the immigrants from the Bauhaus, the most successful were

(Opposite)
University of York, Derwent College: Robert Matthew, Johnson-Marshall and Partners (1964–5)

Possibly the most complete expression of the Social Architecture Movement and a fitting climax to the International Style. To achieve speed of building the university became a member of the Consortium of Local Authorities Special Programme (CLASP) and, with modifications to make the buildings suitable for residential as well as teaching purposes, created a prefabricated university, with colleges loosely grouped around a large new lake which also acted as a balancing reservoir in the drainage of a water-logged site on the edge of the city of York. The university was designated in 1962, the first undergraduates arrived in the autumn of 1963 and by 1970 it accommodated some 3,000 students. With its central lake and careful landscaping, it is often considered the most successful of the new universities of the sixties, both aesthetically and socially.

Royal College of Physicians, Regents Park, London: Denis Lasdun (1960)

Lasdun wanted the building to 'rhyme' with Nash's neo-classical terraces which are hard by, and so his training in Beaux Arts architecture at the Architecture Association School in London came into force to produce his particular abstraction of neo-classicism. It is classic Corbusian in its separation of functions, the offices and working spaces being accommodated in the main block while the assembly hall is in a separate block of dark brick set at right angles to the main hall and having an interesting warped surface. Many consider this Lasdun's finest building – materials are carefully chosen, details impeccable, craftsmanship superb.

Handwritten note on image: Mies van der Rohe - International Style / Less is more

Marcel Breuer and Mies van der Rohe. Breuer had been one of its first students. He quickly became a member of staff and acquired a reputation first as a brilliant designer of standardized modular furniture. His tubular steel furniture was marketed internationally. His architecture, in which he was increasingly occupied, had the same qualities of clarity and definition through the expression of functions. As a teacher, Breuer's influence was profound; his pupils at Harvard included many of the leading American architects of the next generation.

It was Mies van der Rohe, Gropius' successor, who became the most famous and longest surviving representative of the International Style from the Bauhaus. The simplicity and elegance of the buildings that came from his studio captured the imagination of students and practitioners throughout the world. 'Less is more', was his most famous aphorism but that applied to the appearance of simplicity rather than to the size of a building or the design of its detail. His buildings for the Illinois Institute of Technology, which included the School of Architecture, could hardly look simpler; his apartments at Lake Shore Drive in Chicago are so disciplined as to be almost impersonal; his Seagram Building in New York is the

Lovell Health House, Griffith Park, Los Angeles: Richard Neutra (1927–9)

Neutra came to America in 1923. His architectural background can be gleaned from the fact that he worked with Adolph Loos, Otto Wagner and Eric Mendelsohn and met Frank Lloyd Wright at Sullivan's funeral. In 1926 he brought International Modern to the west coast when he set up in partnership in California with Rudolph Schindler. The steel skeleton of the Lovell House was filled with prefabricated glass and concrete panels, and erected on the site in an incredible 40 hours. The sense that the house is clinging by arms and toenails to the sheer side of the ravine in which it is sited is further emphasized by the slabs and balconies blatantly hung from steel cables.

most complete expression of his aesthetic – a brown and bronze rectilinear, elegant slab, set back from the road so that its clean purity could be easily seen.

In America the influence of Mies van der Rohe is everywhere apparent. For example, the most prolific firm of architects celebrated for their work in the International Style is that of Skidmore, Owings and Merrill. Their Lever House in New York, with its glass slab of offices separated and reaching up from a horizontal podium with public and social spaces, became the prototype for hundreds of office blocks in many parts of the world. In all of them, the influence of Mies van der Rohe was the most profound. The tall steel structures (apparently of steel even if actually of reinforced concrete) with flat roofs and refined exterior detailing were his legacy – a mannerism easy to copy and later detested as dry and unimaginative and ultimately boring.

In South America, the architecture was more dramatic but inspired by the same masters. The main influence there was Le Corbusier who was invited to Rio de Janeiro in 1936 as consultant to the architects of the new Ministry of Education building. The *brise-soleil* screen shading the glass wall was a typically Corbusian – and typically influential – solution to the problem of sunlight. After the Second World War, the new capital of Brazilia offered an unprecedented opportunity for spectacular architectural design. The government complex at the centre was an expression of elementary modern principles. The shapes of the units housing the three functions – of assembly, senate and administration – are

Tubular Chair: Marcel Breuer

'Where else but here in Weimar was a generation, struggling to self-expression, offered the possibility of developing its creative powers?' asked van Doesburg. Breuer came to the Weimar Bauhaus as a student of 18, and at 22 took over the furniture department. After working in a variety of woods, he is said to have conceived the idea of using tubular steel in furniture from contemplating the handle-bars of his bicycle as he rode around. He devized a series of chairs in this material (revolutionary as a component of furniture design), some with slung leather seats, and these became prototypes of modern tubular steel furniture. 'He achieved,' says Gillian Naylor, 'the structural lightness, resilience and anonymity he had aimed at in wood.'

St John's Abbey Church, Collegeville, Minnesota: Marcel Breuer (1953–61)

Breuer was now well advanced in his career, producing a spate of college buildings all over America, offices and factories in Europe, town-planning schemes in South America and Asia. This was his busiest and most prolific period. His hallmark again appears in identifying the door in a concrete and glass façade, patterned like wire-mesh by a great placard of concrete hoisted on splayed concrete legs.

Seagram Building, New York

(Opposite)

Seagram Building, 375 Park Avenue, New York: Mies van der Rohe (1954–8)

The impressive presence of the Seagram Building, now one of a street of skyscrapers in Park Avenue, is largely due to its uncompromising simplicity – an unadulterated bronze-glass slab: only symmetrical pools and a canopy on stilts lead one to the entrance. This, too, was a seminal building, but much less happily than the Farnsworth House, for many imitators have ignored texture, quality and proportion in producing

the gargantuan. Walls are curtain walls, that is, not load-bearing but hung on the steel frame. The construction allows an all-purpose building whose interior space can be changed around at will. The interiors are by Philip Johnson.

Farnsworth House, near Plano, Illinois: Mies van der Rohe (1946–50)

An elongated glass pavilion on 12 slim, steel stilts, Mies' work became the pattern for *avant garde* domestic architecture. Some of its progeny such as Philip Johnson's Glass House

in Connecticut or Charles Eames' House at Santa Monica exploited the form to give even greater interaction with the environment. Mies, who had arrived in the States in 1938, was a master of simplicity of elements, fitting his slogan that 'less is more'. Functional divisions between rooms and areas inside this 'poem in glass and steel' are indicated by partitions often made by ceiling to floor curtaining in gathered ribs of natural-coloured silk. This arrangement has been reproduced across the world for offices, discussion and meeting rooms in domestic, commercial and educational institutions.

clearly defined and separate, as the CIAM might have demanded. The popularity of the city as a whole, with its rows of high parallel blocks, has waned – an architect's dream, it has been said, that paid little attention to the needs of people.

The collapse of the International Style can be studied through the architecture of one of its most successful protagonists. Philip Johnson started late as an architect, having been an art historian at the Museum of Modern Art in New York and co-author, with Henry-Russell Hitchcock, of the 1932 book, *The International Style*. An effective publicist for the style, and much influenced by Mies van der Rohe, Johnson took up architectural practice in his forties and built his own house in Cambridge, Mass. His Glass

Lever House, Park Avenue, New York: Skidmore, Owings & Merrill (1951)

Situated almost opposite Mies's Seagram Building, this was Park Avenue's first glass skyscraper, and New York's second. The chief designer was Gordon Bunshaft. A smooth slab block of blue-green glass set between stainless steel strips rises from the podium which houses offices. It has a courtyard at ground level and a roof terrace on top. On its 25th anniversary, the *New York Times* eulogized it as 'the first streamlined office building of gleaming glass and steel with a plaza, a breathing space, so that in the canyons of the city there would be a place for the sun to shine.' The technology of its services set an international standard.

John Hancock Tower, Chicago: Skidmore, Owings & Merrill (1970)

This partnership, formed in the mid-'30s, excelled themselves in skyscrapers in Chicago, New York and San Francisco. This glass tower, reducing in size as it soars smoothly upwards and distinguished by gigantic criss-crossing struts, was designed by a Chicago man also largely responsible for the Sears Tower, Bruce Graham. 'In the heartland we believe in a direct relationship between work and thought,' he says. 'We make real buildings, we are not abstract about life, as they are in New York.'

Brasilia, Brazil: Oscar Niemeyer and Lucio Costa (1956–60)

The new capital of Brazil, set high at 584 miles north-west of Rio de Janeiro, has been called by one critic 'a compendium of the clichés of 20th-century architecture'. Costa won the competition and planned the city on two intersecting axes – in the shape of an aeroplane with curved wings. Niemeyer joined Costa's office as a student, and became chief architect for Brasilia in the late '60s. The main buildings are geometric concrete shapes set at the points of a central triangle. There is a pair of 28-storey towers pointing up like fingers and linked by galleries at certain floors; there is a Senate Building and Assembly Building, both with saucer-shaped features, one upside down; and there is Niemeyer's Cathedral with its pre-cast concrete limbs resembling a roast crown of lamb, probably the best building there. There are hospitals, schools, a theatre, apartment blocks for government officials. As at Chandigarh, the scheme fell short of providing ordinary workers' housing, so shanty towns grew up around, and it has been said that the great city becomes dead after business hours, while all life shifts to the shanty towns.

Glass House, New Canaan, Connecticut: Philip Johnson (1949)

Johnson, probably the best known disciple of Mies van der Rohe and still practising in 1987, moved from Classics to Architecture at Harvard after a Damascene conversion to the Modern Movement on reading an article by Henry Russell Hitchcock. He was the first director of the architectural section of the Museum of Modern Art in New York. Johnson's glass house takes the glass box of the Farnsworth House to its limits so that it virtually disappears altogether. The stilt legs have been eliminated and replaced by an unobtrusive foundation of slim brick

House at New Canaan, Connecticut of 1949 was directly influenced by Mies van der Rohe's glass-enclosed Farnsworth House in Illinois of 1945. After a succession of huge commissions for office blocks, he collaborated with Mies van der Rohe on the Seagram Building.

At the same time he was trying a variety of other styles, culminating in the public eye with his A T & T building in New York, capped with a huge broken pediment that earned it the title of the 'Chippendale Building'. It has the merit of once again creating a lively element in the skyline of New York, which was variegated before the War and got lost among the dreary flat roofs of the International Style. So Johnson, at first its prophet, became its destroyer, watching its demise and entertaining us as a brilliant performer with wit rather than conviction.

The achievement of the International Style was that, with certain limitations, it was indeed international. It was at its best in Western Europe, the United States, occasionally in Soviet Russia, South America and briefly in Japan. Because it aimed to be international it had to be devoid of those local or regional characteristics developed to meet the needs of a local climate that give buildings their individual character. In order to be relevant to all men and all women it had to be simple, uncluttered, repetitive and modular; the ornament that expressed local style or personal eccentricity was eliminated. As the devices to deal with the effects of weathering disappeared, it became an architecture of sheer sides and flat roofs.

Ultimately, the International Style was a conscious style created by artists rather than an inevitable expression of functional need. It was the product of an industrial society with social concern. It spread across the world partly through Le Corbusier, more through the architects who had worked with and for him. It suffered from the faults of its own pedigree. It was intended to be an expression of democracy; it became instead an expression of totalitarianism because it could not avoid expressing the paternalism of its somewhat arrogant expositors. Intended to be good for all individuals, it became good for the anonymous mass in which the individual need and aspiration is forgotten. Its ultimate expression was therefore mass housing – its monument and its sepulchre.

courses; the white lines of the frame have been blackened so that they virtually melt away; furthermore, since one can see right through the house, reflexions of foliage melt into the greenery on the far side, and the box appears saturated with the environment. The services are hidden in an unobtrusive brick cylinder.

Tuberculosis Sanatorium, Paimio, Finland: Alvar Aalto (1929–33)

This sanatorium, and the one by Duiker at Zonnestraal, Hilversum, Holland (which Aalto saw the year before starting work on Paimio) remind us that tuberculosis was the scourge of the time, and that cold, fresh air was considered an essential part of the treatment – 'a tuberculosis sanatorium is to all intents and purposes a house with open windows'. So Paimio was built with the aid and co-operation of 48 communities and four cities, in an area of woods and lakes about 20 miles from Helsinki. Aalto paid much attention to orientation, lighting and heating, and used no mechanical ventilation except in the kitchen areas for which he installed a cleverly zoned system he had re-worked from Duiker's extractor stack at Zonnestraal. The plan shows a series of blocks of different lengths and shapes, following the contours of the site and attached to circulation hallways at different angles, so as to 'funnel you towards the door'. There were three main components: a row of doctors' houses, separate from the rest; a public block encompassing examination, therapy and operating rooms situated next to the service blocks which contained kitchens, bakery and heating plant, etc; and the long six-storey ward block itself. This last was designed particularly with the welfare of long-term patients in mind. All the rooms face south; floors are cantilevered out and there is access to an open roof-terrace partially shielded by a canopy. Radiant heating in the ceiling is directed to the patients' feet, not the head; the wall behind the patients' heads is soft-surfaced; and light fittings cast light for reading so as to not tax eyesight. Substantial changes have been made to translate the sanatorium into a general hospital, but Aalto's clear vision of a sparkling environment for living people (who happen to be sick) has been retained.

CHAPTER NINE

HARMONIOUS LIVING

At the second CIAM (*Congrès Internationaux d'Architecture Moderne*) at Frankfurt in 1929 a young Finnish architect made his first appearance upon the international scene. He was, at that time, far from being an international figure himself. Born in 1898 he came from a forestry village in central Finland. He had designed an office block for a newspaper in Turku and won a competition for a sanatorium in Paimio. He was good company, talked to everyone he met, especially non-architects, had no time for architectural theories (which must have made him a bizarre figure among the theorists of CIAM), wrote few letters and kept no diaries. Interested in everything to do with his country, he had no interest in politics and never voted in elections. He was a totally devoted architect, devoted, that is, to developing an architecture based on human needs and designed for what he called 'harmonious living in a community'. He was Alvar Aalto and his architecture, despite his own shrinking from fame, was celebrated in his own lifetime by a museum devoted to his work. He can be seen as embodying the best qualities that the architecture of the 20th century has revealed.

It may not be an accident that such an individual architecture should appear in such an individual country. Finland is a land of forests and lakes (60,000 lakes in five systems, with outlets to the sea), with industries that are not concentrated in great cities but in smaller groups – places where timber could be floated down for turning into wood pulp and where hydro-electric power would be readily available. Until 1809 it was part of the Swedish kingdom; then after the Russian-Swedish war it became part of the Russian Empire. But it quickly became an autonomous Grand Duchy. The Czar, having decided that the capital Turku was too far from St Petersburg (now Leningrad), Helsinki, then a very small town, became the capital in 1812. Finland obtained its full independence in 1917. Despite wars against both Russia and Germany in the 20th century, it retains its independence.

By the end of the 19th century and the beginning of the 20th,

Finland, like most European countries, was enjoying a revival of national art and culture. Its folk epics inspired artists and writers and its vernacular architecture was being studied and recorded. Its musicians included the greatest of its composers, Sibelius (1865–1957).

In that period of excitement, the publication of H. H. Richardson's architecture and the influence of his American Shingle Style through the work of G. F. Boberg sparked off in Finland, as it had in neighbouring Scandinavian countries, a native architecture whose style is generally described as *national romanticism*. In Sweden, the style was brilliantly represented by Ragnar Ostberg's Stockholm City Hall of 1904–23 and in Denmark, by P. V. Jensen-Klint's Gruntvig Church. In Finland, the leading architects were Lars Sonck (whose massive stone Telephone Company Building of 1903–5 shows the unmistakable influence of Richardson), and Saarinen, Lindgren and Gesellius who won the competition for Helsinki's central station in 1904 and produced the grandest possible symbol of the importance and excitement of railway travel. Saarinen was, in due course, to emigrate to America where he and his son became leading architects of the Modern Movement.

Alvar Aalto built up his practice by winning a succession of architectural competitions. He was an inveterate competition winner. His first two major jobs – the Paimio Sanatorium and the library at Viipuri (destroyed during the 1939–45 war but reconstructed later) were won in competition and he continued to compete throughout his career. Those two initial projects established a way of working but, more importantly, he continued their characteristics, with variations, into his other projects, so identifying him as a major figure in modern architecture – but not in the International Style.

The Paimio Sanatorium, for patients with tuberculosis, contains so many characteristic inventions that it is worth pausing on it to understand something of Aalto's approach to architecture. The wards are on one side of a long straight block which is unusual in construction and planned so that patients get maximum sunlight and air. To make the atmosphere more informal and relaxed Aalto divided the wards internally to form small units for two patients. Every detail, including the wash-hand basins, the lights and the colours of the ceiling and walls were thought out afresh and with concern for comfort. An ingenious detail of the windows ensured that there would be ample natural ventilation without artificial means or controls. The doctors' houses were placed so that they could not see the main hospital and could therefore put their work out of their minds when they were at home.

In the library, there was top-lighting carefully designed so that

City Hall, Hantverkargaten, Stockholm: Ragner Ostberg (1904–23)

The upsurge of the Scandinavian Romantic Movement in the 20th century makes the Town Hall into a palace full of echoes of a rich and royal past. The elevation to the river has an arcade reminiscent of Venetian palaces running right along at ground floor level; above are the regular windows to the long gallery. The river façade seems longer and lower by virtue of the slim and impressive tall tower. It has two internal courtyards; an open Civic Court and the covered Blue Hall (all the rooms have high-sounding names). The main audience chambers are on the first floor in correct *piano nobile* style, and progress to any main chamber is redolent of approaching the throne-room and the presence in a royal palace – a stately ceremonial procession through round and cubic rooms, along the long gallery overlooking the river, through arches 40 feet high.

Central Station, Rautatientori, Helsinki: Eliel Saarinen (1907–14)

The competition was, in fact, won by the partnership of Saarinen, Lindgren and Gesellius but in the six years before it was built, the designs were almost totally re-worked by Saarinen. Saarinen, the father of the Kennedy Airport architect, had in the meantime travelled in Europe and visited Josef Olbrick at Darmstadt and also Peter Behrens, and a strong influence of Jugenstihl-into-Bauhaus has entered to rout Swedish Romanticism. This is then a seminal building, marking the transition from Scandinavian Romanticism to Modern. The sense of presence about the entry façade recalls the grandeur and excitement of train travel which the 19th-century architects built into their railway stations. For where

Finnish country stations still bear the mark of a country that was for one hundred years a Grand Duchy of Russia, this station has the air of an important building in the capital of an independent country. The long, symmetrical façade (marred only by the tall thin tower on the far corner which fits ill with the design) is centrally cut into by the huge semi-circular arch of the entry, the arch chamfered back and finished off with a delicate pie-crimped edge. All the detailing on the front is vertical: ranks of tall, thin lights along the façade and on either side of the entry a pair of strong-chinned heroic figures, staring impassively ahead, and holding in their hands art nouveau polygonal electric lanterns. The stonework is rugged granite recalling the textures of H. H. Richardson's work in America. The meticulous care with which Saarinen plotted the dimensions of every stone can be seen from the radiating stones round the archway.

the funnel-like forms would diffuse the light without needing diffusing glasses. The hot water pipes were placed between the skylights. The ceiling was made of undulating timber, the result of innumerable diagrams studying sound reflections so that the acoustics would be right for discussions.

In both the hospital and the library, the furniture was specially designed for its purpose. The hospital needed furniture that would be light, washable and hygienic as well as comfortable, so the bent wood furniture was designed and thereafter became a regular Aalto feature. To produce it, he and Maire Gullichsen founded the furniture firm of Artek in 1931, which started with the bent wood furniture and went on to produce glassware, lamps and textiles. For it and the library, the new furniture was designed so that it could become a general item and be suitable for mass production.

Aalto's approach is like a breath of fresh air. In contrast to the principles of CIAM and the International Style, every problem has to be thought out afresh because its solution will come from a study of particular human needs. What can properly be standard-ized is not the whole building, but its smaller components. The furniture can, and indeed must, be standard. Details such as door handles could be either special or general – usually the latter. In short, a good building is individual, inspired by and related to its site, generated by the study of the needs of its potential users.

Another essential aspect of Aalto's work is his attitude to technology. Although not averse to it, he was aware of its dangers, not because it could take over but because it could be the least effective way to solve a simple problem. Aalto's technology is what might nowadays be described as alternative technology. It was the product of his study of human needs and the application of common sense. Why should an architect use an expensive system of controls if there was a simple, more natural and effective way of solving the problem? So, for example, the hospital was naturally ventilated by an original, ingenious window fitting; the ceiling of the library was shaped so that the acoustics would be right without artificial aids, microphones or loudspeakers; houses, like hospital wards, would be orientated so that the views were better and the light and shade be easily controlled if the windows faced the right way.

The variety of buildings that his workshop produced testifies to the variety of his interest and versatility. They included hospitals, libraries, houses and flats, town halls and sports halls, industrial buildings, churches, a few private houses, a university and colleges, schools and concert halls. In the latter part of his life he was responsible for several town plans and regional plans, all revealing the same essential attitude that had characterized the architecture – informality, the study of the site, character without pomposity.

The competitions provided some of the most exhilarating and educational episodes in his workshop. All the staff were architects and there were no draughtsmen; they were expected to work through friendly cooperation in a family atmosphere of common endeavour. For in architecture, he considered, there are no solitary problems. Everything is related to everything else; and nothing must be allowed to relapse into mere routine. The work produced by the office was inspired by the same commitments that inspired his earliest buildings – concern for the individual rather than the mass, the setting, the use of technics in the service of man – in short a profound humanism. He saw nature and man as one, and was clear about the continuity of both. Human life consists, he thought, in equal degrees of tradition and new creation. Continuity is a vital necessity.

Bent Wood Chair: Alvar Aalto

Finland's basic material – wood – early suggested itself to Aalto for furniture making. An early wooden structure is dedicated by Aino and Alvar Aalto to 'Henry van de Velde, the great pioneer of architecture of our times; the first to envisage the revolution in the techniques of wood.' Aalto says the first experiments 'consisted of trying to bend laminated structures in one direction. It was always my dream to know how to create multi-dimensional, sculptural forms in wood, which would eventually lead to freer and more stable forms.' Instead of conventional steaming methods he experimented with laminating and bending via the natural moisture in birch. Designs were usually directed towards a particular building. The first furniture was made for the Sanatorium at Paimio, to find a softer, less cold material than steel that was more malleable to the human body, for the comfort of the tubercular patients. An experimental workshop was set up, out of which grew Artek furniture. By the time he was creating the all-wooden furniture for the library at Viipuri, he was talking of conceiving furniture not only suitable for that particular project, but which would also be susceptible to mass production.

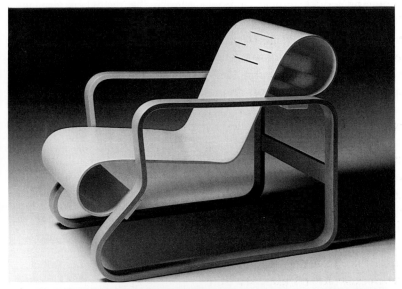

Glass Vase: Alvar Aalto

The most common artefact for architects to get involved with is furniture, particularly chairs. Aalto's talents stretched across the board, designing ventilation systems, light fittings and glass objects.

In that sense, Aalto represents the nearest I can discover to the integration of the themes which I have been extracting in this study. He was first and last concerned with the understanding of nature; he knew the vernacular of his country; he believed in the continuity of buildings and the land; he studied the behaviour of light and sound; he designed for comfort – harmonious living in a community. And he was a superb manipulator of space. He was concerned to bring those factors together in a recognizable unity, though it was not an obvious conventional unity. He believed, to quote a friend, in 'a unified conception, unified design and a unified way of life'. It was not a formal, and certainly not a symmetrical, unity.

The key to his style can be seen in the plans of his buildings which are quite distinctive. He seems often to have started with the shape of the 'L'. Then there are parallel blocks, often staggered and open at the ends. In contrast to those elements, or growing from them, he introduces a distinctive shape, sometimes projecting from the side to house a special function. Alternatively, he makes the overall plan a fan-shape or like the fingers of a hand spreading out from the palm. The plans are thus anthropomorphic and open to nature, and the parallel forms are slid together so that the whole complex is tightly unified.

Against that background it is necessary to refer only briefly to a selection of his more famous works. The cellulose factory at Sunila was built between 1935 and 1939. In contrast to what was expected, Aalto did not level the site but used the natural rock formation to ensure that it steps down to the harbour. The components of the factory are clearly expressed, partly by using different materials – brick for the production buildings, white concrete for the transport buildings. The houses for the factory employees are laid out following the contours and slopes so that each house has direct access to natural ground without staircases.

His unusual approach to the planning of a large building can be seen in the dormitory he designed for the Massachusetts Institute of Technology. It has a strange kind of unity for on one side the elevations are flat, broken only by the distinctive cantilevering of the stairs that run up the side of the block. On the other side they form an undulating wall so that all the rooms facing that way have slightly different aspects.

What is often regarded as his most seminal building was the house Aalto designed, with remarkable care and thought and revision, for an industrialist who was also an art patron and his wife, who was an artist. That was the Villa Mairea (1938–9). He used the characteristic L-plan, with the forest forming a wall to complete the courtyard, and he introduced another device which he repeated many times – the use of moveable internal walls. The ground floor is one large room with moveable partitions so that it

Baker Dormitory, Massachusets Institute of Technology, Cambridge Massachusets: Alvar Aalto (1947–9)

During the European slump in building occasioned by the War, Aalto had made part of his living by lecturing trips to Massachusets Institute of Technology, and through this he gained the commission for the dormitory block. On the principle that scenery looks better seen sideways (as from a moving train), he planned the block in a sinuous Z-shape so that rooms have views up and down the Charles River which borders the site, and none are directly at right angles to the roadway. The block utilizes good red Boston brick and is punched with all-over fenestration.

Cellulose Factory and Workers' Housing, Sunila: Alvar Aalto (1935–9)

This is an early large-scale work, built for his industrial friends, Harry and Maire Gullichsen. Sunila is a rocky island in the Gulf of Finland near the port of Kotka and shelters five large industrial enterprises. The rock face falls steeply to deep water, allowing boats to anchor without need of a harbour. Aalto therefore organized the factory layout so that the process would start at the top of the rock, and each stage of the manufacture would work its way down to a lower level, so that the finished product arrived at the boats. The complex has a pyramid-shaped outline. The administrative offices and laboratories in red brick are set on the topmost terrace of the Baltic granite site, complete with peaceful gardens (the bridge of the ship from which the entire production process can be overseen and directed) and

then the work operates through a series of buildings, also in brick, down the levels of the hill to the long, low white concrete warehouse at the water's edge. Original trees were retained and open parkland walks connect buildings, so that workers immediately on leaving work can be absorbed with nature. The housing is across an inlet, built on the south slopes only of a rolling, hilly area, while the original forest was retained on the north slopes. Where units are one on top of each other, there are separate entries on upper and lower levels, removing the need for stairs.

could be a living room or a gallery lined with pictures. The roof is supported by steel columns wrapped with leather bands and the walls are finished in teak or Finnish fir with parapets of grey granite. The roof of the wing leading to the sauna and the outside pool is covered with grass. But what made the villa utterly memorable and marks it out as a seminal building of the Modern Movement was its manipulation of space. By the simplest of articulations, the placing of an open staircase, slight changes in level from the entrance to different parts of the plan, the space is ever changing, sensitively lit and very harmonious.

The villa also demonstrated one of the essential aspects of Aalto's approach to design, which is also central to modern architecture. The main functions in the interior – the volumes and spaces – are expressed on the exterior. That is achieved through the geometry which, with its surprises, makes the observer wonder what can be happening inside and through the varying materials drawing attention to the different spaces. It might be argued that one of the most distinctive characteristics of modern architecture is that, without the use of traditional decorative motifs or ornament, the building is able to tell you what is happening inside and stimulate your curiosity to enter – a journey of constant discovery and surprise.

The building that illustrates most vividly these attitudes is also generally regarded as the most attractive and humane of all Aalto's works. The Town Hall at Säynätsalo, won in a competition in 1949 and built between 1950 and 1952, sits on a rugged island in Lake Päijänne and serves a community of some 3,000 people, all dependent upon one industry. While Aalto was responsible for the layout of the town the main complex is the Town Hall, with its offices, council chamber, a library and a number of apartments. He used earth from the foundations to make a plaza raised above the level of the rest of the site and surrounded it with buildings of local red brick with copper roofing.

The council chamber is almost a cube. Aalto's knowledge and understanding of the behaviour of timber enabled him to devise a memorable roof structure of triangulated frames with struts spraying out from timber pads to support the secondary framing of the roof. Outside, the profiles of the building units add up to one of the most satisfying groups of dignified, but unpretentious, social buildings it is possible to imagine. The steps leading to the plaza are straight at one side of the complex and rhythmically informal at the other.

It is difficult to do justice to this singular architect's individual but never arrogant style. Among his other buildings that illustrate the same points are his pavilion for the New York World Fair in 1939 with its sloping jettied wooden walls and free architectural form demonstrating as much as the exhibits Finland's country,

Villa Mairea, Noormarkku, Finland: Alvar Aalto (1938–9)

A 19th-century industrial enterprise had been set up in this area of pine forest in West Finland, and there were already big houses in the area in Victorian and Art Nouveau style built for the original factory owners. Aalto and his wife Aino designed their greatest domestic triumph for their friends the industrialists Harry and Maire Gullichsen. On a hilltop overlooking forest and with glimpses of a saw-mill, the house typifies Aalto's ability to combine technical practicality with a deep sympathy for the location and his client's needs: it is built to live the good life in that particular place. It has the inevitable Finnish sauna with a kidney-shaped pool beside it – a concrete shell floating, without foundations, on the subsoil. The outline of the house is far from regular with the rounded trapezoidal shape, slatted in wood, of Mrs Gullichsen's first-floor studio jutting out over an entry porch supported on poles simply lashed together. Art and everyday life intermix: the moveable partitions which can transform the open living space for exhibitions are in fact cupboards in which the paintings can be stored. Of the two dining-rooms in the east wing stretching out to the forest, one is for the long snow months of winter, the other, the summer one, doubles as a verandah. Venetian blinds on the outside of the house control sunlight and because the Finnish summer has long months when darkness for sleeping lasts only a few hours, the bedroom windows are all small and slanted away from the rising sun.

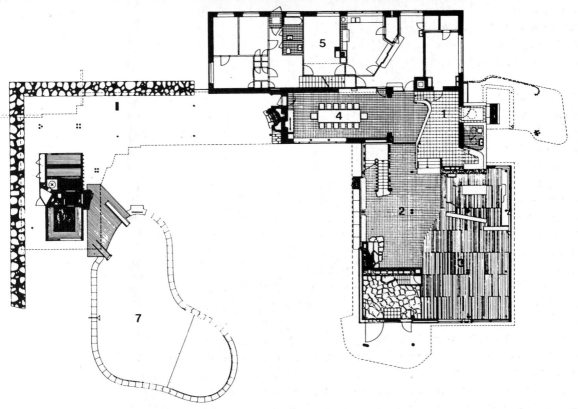

Town Hall steps, Säynätsalo: Alvar Aalto (1950–2)

Säynätsalo was a new town in central Finland. Like many of his works, Aalto won this commission by competition. The buildings are grouped round courtyards and terraces which have now become very overgrown. But Aalto may not have regretted this: some of his designs for the Baker Dormitories in Massachusets show his buildings embowered in trellises and greenery.

Aesthetic, practical and structural aims come together in the roof of the tiny Council Chamber. Finnish winters require a ventilated roofspace, so the structural supports are exposed inside the hall – the triangular struts arranged in a series of exciting sunbursts along the ceiling.

Institute of Technology, Otaniemi, Espoo, Helsinki: Alvar Aalto (1955–64)

This was another competition success when, in 1949, it was decided to move the hundred year old Finnish Technical University to Otaniemi, a wooded peninsula across a bay in the suburbs of Helsinki. Aalto placed his buildings towards the back of the diamond-shaped site, away from two motorways which hemmed in it. Aalto made the master plan but designed only the main building and a few laboratories himself. The main building stands on the raised central site of the original great house of the estate. It houses administrative areas and a series of lecture theatres of different capacities, each characterized by Aalto's beautiful working and finish of woods and by indirect glare-free sunlight introduced through strip lighting. Other than the curved plan of the main auditorium there is no relation to the outer appearance

people, work and products; the church at Imatra with moveable internal walls of concrete to make either one or three spaces; the civic buildings and library at Seinajoki of 1961–5 with its fan-shaped library wall; the Polytechnic buildings at Otaniemi with curving assembly hall and theatre; the apartment block at Bremen with its irregular fan-shaped plan so that the rooms are all different. The windows look out from the long wall and the sharp end of the block seems to say that nothing is static but points always to nature outside.

In a rare talk entitled *An Architect's Conscience* in 1957, Aalto explained some of his convictions about architecture. He saw everything in a great continuity. Living quarters were dependent upon the city, the city upon the region. Human needs could be studied and met with a view to fostering harmonious living within a community.

In the pursuit of that objective, he was fully aware of the predicament of modern architecture. He recognized that the housing problem is without doubt one of the most important to be solved – and it is intractable. The need for the privacy of the family and the need for housing in a densely packed great city will never,

dominated by an open amphitheatre, clearly influenced by those of Greece (Aalto sketched the one at Delphi in 1953). Its smooth, triangular screen walls, built from specially-made red brick on a curving steel frame, sweep down from the sky with the panache and flourish of a Shakespearian courtier doffing his hat. Sadly it is little used, for the snow scarcely melts from the stage area before the students go down for the long summer vacation.

Finnish Pavilion, New York World Fair: Alvar Aalto (1939)

Aalto cheated by secretly sending in two designs for this competition, and since his wife with even greater secrecy entered a third, his office won all three prizes. Aalto wanted to combine the requirements of rationality with the symbolism of the Finnish countryside and display Finland to the maximum within the constriction of a small site. The pavilion is 52 feet high and four storeys in all, and the display is conceived vertically sometimes going right up the wall in horizontal strips, like a building façade. Such is the rippling wall of photographs in layers which from top to bottom exhibit at the top: COUNTRY; below: PEOPLE; below: WORK; and, along the bottom: PRODUCTS. Every bit of the Pavilion was treated as a display; wall surfaces of wood were treated in different ways to be themselves exhibits; pressed wood aeroplane propellers (which were a proud Finnish export) were slung from the ceiling and worked as fans for ventilation. 'An exhibition,' said Aalto, 'should be what in the early days it used to be, a general store in which all possible objects are grouped together in a dense display – whether it be fish, cloth or cheese. Therefore, in this pavilion I have attempted to provide the densest possible concentration of display, a space filled with wares, next to and above and beneath each other, agricultural and industrial products often just a few inches apart. It was no easy work – composing the individual elements into one symphony.'

he thought, be resolved. Should people live in isolated or compact groups? We live two lives – collective and private. Was it possible for life in a high-rise culture to approximate to that in a small private house?

In that question, he posed one of the fundamental problems for the contemporary designer with a social conscience – a problem which has caused unhappiness when it was not faced, where sheer scale took over from the study of human needs. He believed that harmonious living in a house was the principle that must be satisfied. In the big apartment block in the Hansaviertel in Berlin of 1957 he got as close to achieving it as anyone has, with rooms grouped round open air rooms or patios and the block slightly bent in the centre, open at the ground floor for ease of access. It did what he wanted – compensated to some extent for the inevitable lack of contact between the house and the natural environment. He was attempting to unify man and nature – a recurring theme in our secular society. Aalto's influence was pervasive – at first in Finland, then world-wide. 'He traced out', to quote his most celebrated follower Reima Pietilä, 'a philosophy of geographical localism in the early thirties. He was certainly the first in our country to exploit Finnish landscape as a direct source for design form.'

Born in Turku in 1923, Pietilä, like Aalto, built up a practice through competitions and has taken further the exploration and exploitation of organic form. His teaching is difficult and influential, his architecture various but always provocative. His Kaleva church at Tampere was 'an experiment in convex-concave morphology'; the Dipoli Centre in the Institute of Technology at Otaniemi 'a morphological exercise into the mineral world' (in concrete); the Finnish Embassy in New Delhi has 'white roofing shaped as in snow sculpted by the wind'; and the 1987 Official Residence of the President of Finland expresses the 'mythological forces of the Finnish nature: receding glaciation and subsequent land upheavals.'

Apartment block, Hansaviertel, Berlin: Alvar Aalto (1955–9)

The Interbau Exhibition after the War in Berlin was an exhibition with a difference – the housing was commissioned from internationally recognized architects and was built to last and to be lived in. Aalto aimed to combine the community advantages he saw in apartment building with those of privacy and personal ownership given by small private housing developments. The corridor-balconies common in European blocks of flats therefore became patios with each flat's rooms grouped round. Such compromises may be what laid him open to criticisms that his architecture is '... essentially ... not open to urban typologies' (Manfredo Tafuri and Frencesco Dal Co., 1976). It produced unusually spacious-feeling rooms full of light and 'open air'. On one side, entry is on two levels, the lower leading to lifts, and bicycle and pram parks, the upper to an open-air terraced vestibule sheltered by a canopy which was to serve as a common meeting place for tenants, and from which a ramp led to the children's playground.

CHAPTER TEN

THE EXPRESSION OF TECHNOLOGY

Spatial Design and Structures

In all the recognized authoritative histories of modern architecture it has always been an accepted article of faith that the modern movement depended on – or was caused by – or reflected changes in – the development of structural engineering in the 19th and 20th centuries. In that development, two materials or systems were definitive. Once it had become possible to use steel instead of cast- or wrought iron, vast new possibilities in framed buildings were opened up. Similarly, the development of reinforced concrete, first as conventional concrete reinforced by steel bars and then made stronger and more sophisticated by the introduction of pre-stressing, enlarged design possibilities. It was not only used in Europe and America where steel was reasonably plentiful but also in countries where steel was available in limited quantities.

The difficulty with this historical account is that some of the most original and experimental buildings of the era, including many of those described in the early chapters of this book, did not use such materials at all. The architects' visions seem frequently to have become enlarged and original with entirely traditional materials, sometimes (as in the work of the Arts and Crafts architects) used in a traditional way, sometimes (in work such as that of Gaudi) in an entirely new way. Two aspects of the new architecture were, however, dependent upon the new technology – the ability to create bigger and more interpenetrating volumes in the interior, and the ability to go higher than ever before.

Those were the positive virtues of the new possibilities; and they were seized with alacrity and energy. The negative aspect was the constraints that for many years seemed to reduce the imaginative possibilities of the new structures. The reason is simple. Steel and reinforced concrete used carefully and conscientiously but without adventure led to a rectilinear architecture which could be

Exhibition Hall, Turin: Pier Luigi Nervi (1948–50)

Since 1927 Nervi had been building bridges and viaducts, tanks and silos by calculation. But his pre-occupation and experiments with structures based on natural forms ('strength through form') first bore fruit in the Exhibition Hall in Turin. In a speedy eight months there rose a rectangular building with strip windows, covered by a revolutionary rippling roof of cast concrete panels, supported on a concrete vault springing from the ground. Although

analyzed in three dimensions reduced to two – length, and breadth and depth. The dimensions, then, were calculated in terms of three kinds of structural behaviour – tension, compression and bending. The mathematics of structural engineering was most readily checked with buildings that were orthogonal and rectilinear – in short, elementary. The technology of steel and concrete was, therefore, a major factor in forcing modern architecture into boxes.

There was nothing wrong about that. Steel and concrete were capable of enormous development and led to some stunning structures – and still do. The fantastic towers of Manhattan would have been impossible without it. The crowded cities of the Third World could only be developed with such structures. But modern architecture was not dependent upon them. What made modern architecture more exciting than ever before – and created a new dimension never before exploited on such a scale – was the structure not of regular geometry and calculated mathematics but of spatial design, warped surfaces and interlocking units. Ultimately, such design would be seen finding its imagination in nature. It is to that wealth of structures that we must now turn and, in particular, to four leading exponents of the style.

Pier Luigi Nervi (1891–1979) was the most celebrated exponent of the structural principle, describing it as 'strength through

a misunderstanding on the part of the builders changed the form of the apse from Nervi's design, nevertheless the enormous single span, carried on ribs that spring from forked buttresses, is highly exciting. Nervi's aim had been to evolve a process to create 'load-bearing shells ... to be built rapidly and economically ... by subdividing the proposed surfaces into sections of 20–40 square feet and to fabricate each of these sections in a mould, so that when assembled they create the desired surface. The edges of the sections are so shaped that when they are set near one another they create the forms in which to lay the reinforcing bars and to pour the concrete of the stiffening ribs four to five inches wide. The sectional elements are reinforced with steel mesh. The subdivision of the surface into sectional elements is completely free, so that the stiffening ribs create an interesting and highly expressive geometric pattern.'

form', or strength through shape. Trained in engineering at Bologna University and Professor of Structural Engineering for many years in the Faculty of Architecture at the University of Rome, he represents a rare understanding of the unity and mutual interaction of architecture and engineering. It was not that he avoided or despised calculation; indeed, he recognized the beauty of precise calculations of structures. But he insisted that the beauty of structures is not so much the result of calculation but rather the knowledge of which calculations to use. His work was a continual demonstration of intuitive knowledge based on experience.

The Communal Stadium in Florence of 1930–2 was his first experiment in making an expressive architecture from exposed structural elements. The material was his own modification of reinforced concrete, *ferrocemento*, and with it he was able to make not only buildings but his own sailing boat, the first concrete boat in existence. His structural ingenuity enabled him to span increasingly large areas – for aircraft hangars and most famously for the great Exhibition Hall at Turin of 1948–9, an immense roof composed of prefabricated units whose ribs are elegantly gathered together before reaching down to the ground. This was structure as poetry and Nervi, in lectures and discussions, never failed to emphasize the way in which beauty could be derived from the refinement of structure.

His corpus of structures included the impeccably detailed Palazzetto dello Sport for the Rome Olympics of 1956–7 and the conference hall for UNESCO in Paris in which he collaborated with Marcel Breuer in 1953–7. That is a folded slab, used on the walls and the roof structure, and it reveals a fundamental aspect of Nervi's structural design. He observed that in nature, strength is increased by folded forms, in grasses and palms. Nature also produces vertical cantilevers; trees are effectively vertical can-

Palazzetto dello Sport, Rome: Pier Luigi Nervi (1956–7)

The smaller of two stadia for the Olympic Games of 1960, it holds 5,000 people. It is another example of the new geometries of curved surfaces with which architects were experimenting in the '50s, and because the elements were prefabricated it was built in 40 days. The roof is a shallow dome of 200 feet diameter of shell concrete about two inches thick. Y-shaped supports carry the roof and let light flood in under the dome.

Pirelli Office Block, Milan: Pier Luigi Nervi with Gio Ponti and others (1955–8)

Ponti's work had, until now, been a combination of neo-classical with rationalist and functional influences, as befitted a follower of Otto Wagner. But he and Nervi, in this 33-storey high building beside the railway station in Milan, produced not only one of the earlier skyscrapers in Europe, but one of the first anywhere to diversify on the rectangular block form. Based on a tree, the four supporting stanchions get slimmer as they approach the top; the tower is both tapered and faceted. It has lifts at the core and uses a double vertebrate system instead of the usual steel cage.

tilevers. The structure of the Pirelli Building in Milan, in which he collaborated with Gio Ponti 1955–8, narrows as it rises and is stabilized by the great thickness at the base.

Nervi found structural strength for his shapes throughout nature, combining suppleness and rhythm. He studied mussels and many kinds of shellfish, insects, and animals and flowers, and found a beauty as Gaudi had done, which could be recreated in modern structures. Being both an engineer and a contractor, he could refine and perfect his own methods of prefabrication on site. He was a master of structures made from prefabricated units and his structures could be either continuous, in which the strength of the members is dependent on the integrity of the whole, or calculated, as separate determinate forms, like a forest of separate trees.

Younger than Nervi and overlapping with his career but, as far as I know, never meeting or working with him, Felix Candela (born in 1910), studied in Spain and was involved in the Spanish Civil War before emigrating to Mexico in 1939. Candela was the prime exponent of shell vaults, using concrete in thin membranes to cover large or small areas. His special contribution was his development of the hyperbolic paraboloid, a possibility he observed in nature. The hyperbolic paraboloid has a special advantage in the making of reinforced concrete. It is a sheet warped in two directions so that its opposite corners turn down or up, but it is geometrically composed of straight lines. The covering is shaped or warped, the basic structure is straight.

In the formation of structures which are poured onto timber shuttering, this was a dramatic and economical advantage; while the timber members of the shuttering could be straight, the resulting structure could be curved in several directions. It could also be thin. Candela's first use of the hyperbolic paraboloid was for the Cosmic Ray pavilion in the University of Mexico City. Of his more famous structures, probably the most original and directly inspired by nature was the open air restaurant at Xochimilco and the Church of St Maria Miraculosa in Mexico City, 1954–5. The straight and warped concrete surfaces form a fantastic interior always said to be influenced by Gaudi – a forest of the hyperbolas and parabolas that Gaudi used.

Candela always insisted that his knowledge was intuitive rather than calculated and that he worked by trial and error rather than calculations. In fact, as I have experienced in discussions with him, he has the most detailed knowledge of mathematics and solid geometry.

The third in this quartet of structural designers who brought new shapes into the world was Buckminster Fuller (1895–1983). Fuller was the most delightful, irrepressible and energetic little man whose lectures were thronged by thousands of students

Xochimilco Restaurant, Mexico City: Felix Candela (1957–8)

Candela's magic delicate shell structure replaced a wooden restaurant which had been burnt down. It stands on a promontory between canals carrying flower-laden gondolas in a fairytale garden setting. People call it 'Los Manantiales' – 'the springs' or 'fountains' – and its four intersecting hypars float on the water-logged silt foundations as effortlessly as a lotus flower on a pool. In fact, the distribution of the weight over an area of 150 feet, through invisible umbrella footings at the points where the groins touch down on the silt, is pure genius, as is the creation of the unbroken loops of shell-concrete, like a skipping rope being danced along the ground, which have no edges to reinforce them.

Chapel of San Vincente de Paul, Coyoacan, Mexico: Enrique de la Mora and Fernando Lopez C. Carmona (architects) and Felix Candela (engineer)

This chapel, built for the St Vincent de Paul nuns and the public, is based on the starched white sail-like peasant hat of the time of the order's foundation and worn by the nuns. The hat-roof sits on a plan shaped like a three-pointed star. The roof is

made from three kite-shaped, straight-edged shells, laced together at the top (as a roof-plan shows) across three propeller-shaped glass areas. As in the Xochimilco restaurant, we see how he had achieved his aim of creating shells with the weight so distributed that the smooth edges did not need to be reinforced – an aim he had long pursued: 'If we imagine a shell formed by four pieces of a sphere ... I think it would be possible to leave the outer boundaries of the structure free of any edge force or stress. Loads could go to the supports via the groins or interior edges ... I knew the free edge was a practical idea long before I understood how it worked and dared to build it.'

listening to even more thousands of words as he poured out his comments on everything in the world and outside it. Of his engineering or architectural work, three examples are important in this story. The Dymaxion House of 1927 was a centralized structure incorporating the technical devices he considered necessary for efficient modern life. Its title indicated its meaning: Dymaxion is short for 'dynamic plus maximum efficiency'. The house has never been built but remains an idea which has exerted much influence upon designers in many parts of the world.

Fuller's major contribution was his use of the geodesic dome – again combining prefabrication with shaped elements made of straight members. The domes could be made from octahedrons or, most frequently, from tetrahedrons; Fuller himself patented the use of the dodecahedron. What was the advantage of the geodesic dome? Simply that it could enclose the greatest possible space within the minimum of surface area; and it could use almost any material – metal or plastic or even cardboard. Strength through shape was again paramount. The most famous of Fuller's domes was the US pavilion for Expo '67 at Montreal.

Towards the end of his life, Fuller experimented with what (with characteristic verbal felicity) he called tensegrity structures, in which the compressive rods are held in space by strings in tension. A totally 3-dimensional structure, its full use has not yet been explored; its potentialities are boundless.

The last – and possibly the most influential – architect is Frei Otto, born in 1925. An admirer of the work of both Candela and Fuller, Otto has taken their experiments in spatial geometry and the use of warped surfaces still further. In particular, he recognized the possibilities inherent in the shape of tents which had never been exploited fully in modern times, except for sport and temporary shelters. What does a tent depend upon? Rods and strings – compression members held in place by tensile members. The use of tension structures was one of the great discoveries of our time.

The modern tent is the creation of Frei Otto. He had been a fighter pilot in the Second World War and came to admire the light structure of fighter planes. But it was the skin over the frame that he saw could be used as a component part of the structure, not just as the covering. The traditional tent could be a prototype for adaptable buildings. Some of the most attractive of his early experiments are the riverside pavilions in the city of Cologne erected in 1957, and the most famous was the West German pavilion with its extensive flowing roofscape also for Expo '67 in Montreal.

From tents, Otto went on to develop cable-net roofs, at first simple and then pre-stressed. The first cable-net roofs were used in the Swiss National Exhibition of 1964 at Lausanne. Their use has

Dymaxion House (a project); Richard Buckminster Fuller (1927)

Buckie Fuller, a rotund and cheerful person who never stopped talking and travelled the world into old age to delight audiences of students, architects and non-specialists with his practical, if unorthodox, ideas, insisted that *his* 'machine for living in' (Dymaxion House, an aluminium house with the services stored in a central core mast) was a lot more functional than those of Corbusier and the International Movement.

Geodesic Dome, US Pavilion, World's Fair Expo '67, Montreal: Buckminster Fuller (1967)

This huge dome, 254 feet in diameter – a geodesic structure of triangles and hexagonal elements covered in a plastic skin – is the most famous of these structures which Fuller would construct out of metal, plastic – or even cardboard. Fuller liked domes – not because of some Renaissance worship of the perfect form, but because he was intrigued by the practical possibilities of this kind of shell as a shelter for man, and envisaged that whole communities could live in such a 'benign physical microcosm', in which not only lighting and temperature could be controlled, but even climate.

German Pavilion, Expo '67, Montreal: Frei Otto (1957)

It is interesting that books on modern architecture frequently exclude engineers such as Nervi, Candela, Otto and Fuller although their adventurous structures are among the more positive architectural developments of the time. His Riverside Pavilions for dancing and shelter were early textile forms of the basic Bedouin tent shape which Otto has re-worked in many forms during his career, spawning all sorts of net and rope structures. At Lausanne, Otto moved from small-span, cotton-canvas tent structures to a transitional membrane with cable net, a significant step in his progress to his first pre-stressed cable-net at the German Pavilion at Expo '67. The cable-net principle has been used in open-air theatres, Olympic stadia and hotels, exploiting its possibilities for retraction. Such a retractable structure has been employed by Skidmore, Owings and Merrill in the Hajj airport at Jeddah – a complex of cable-net umbrellas to form a 'building' which is only in use annually during the pilgrimage period.

huge possibilities, especially when the cable-net patterns are, as they can now be, calculated by computer.

The structures designed by, or stimulated by, Frei Otto are extensive and varied. They include the cable-net pavilions, the use of pre-stressed textiles, of grid shells, of retractable roofs on steel cables. It was his investigation of biological phenomena that enabled him to produce startlingly original forms – like his design for a flexible crane, which must have been inspired by a study of the spinal column of animals or humans. Since 1970, he has been investigating natural structures with remarkable results including an important building type – pneumatic structures. Composed of shaped plastic skins held up by air pressure only slightly greater than that outside and virtually unnoticeable to those inside, such a building type has obvious, and much used, advantages (space without supports) for storage of large items of machinery and manufacture.

The structural discoveries of such leading engineers have led to some fascinating buildings. Kenzo Tange's Olympic Stadium for

(Opposite, above)

Olympic Stadium, Tokyo: Kenzo Tange (1964)

This disciple of Le Corbusier used bridge-builders' techniques in his stadium for the Olympic Games in his native country. The roof is slung on long cables and from the outside it sweeps up to be furled round a central protruding rod. Inside, the tent-like sheets are slung from steel cables like an overhead trampoline, seeming to reflect the spirit and vigour of the sporting activities they protect – a fine exercise in imaginative structural gymnastics. In

Tange's architecture, we see the aggressive technological progress developing which characterizes Japan today.

TWA Terminal, Kennedy Airport, New York: Eliel Saarinen (1956–62)

Something happened at Idlewild (now Kennedy) Airport, something dynamic but also symbolic of the flights which were the *raison d'etre* of the building. From concrete, Saarinen modelled a supple, soaring and birdlike creation.

the Tokyo Olympics of 1963 was a superb tensile structure, and Eliel Saarinen's terminal at Kennedy Airport was a brilliant exercise in concrete engineering. And Utzon's Sydney Opera House was the most beautiful of all expressions of structure – like sails billowing on the headland. How ironic that it seems to be a shell structure but is, in fact, a brilliantly calculated series of prefabricated units making a first-rate imitation of shells.

The development of such structural innovations stems from the designers wishing to exploit the possibilities of tension structures, like the great 19th-century engineers with suspension bridges. While conventional engineering science led to the most regular and orthogonal buildings, modern architecture – essentially the architecture of space – needed to be described in terms of three dimensions, not just two. So, structural design moved from suspension to space, from suspension structures to spatial design. The virtues of spatial design were that it could be either statically determinate or continuous. In all aspects it was the study of natural form that had generated this next stage of structural design. What made that possible was the availability of new materials.

Architects in the early years of the 20th century had been excited by D'Arcy Thompson's studies, *Growth and Form*, published in 1919, which revealed through drawings many of the structures discernible in Nature. Now it was possible to recreate them – shells and honeycombs and leaves and water drops could be analysed and brought to life again in man-made structures. This was – and still is – the engineering vision that has placed a family of new, exciting and practical forms in today's environment. The reverse side of that picture is the use by modern architects of what may look like advanced structures, but are, in fact, the image rather than the reality. Of that we shall see more at the end of this study.

Opera House, off Bennalong Point, Sydney: Jørn Utzon (1956–73)

The most spectacular and in many ways the most unsatisfactory of contemporary buildings was the competition-winning design of a young Danish architect who had no large-scale work behind him. The long drawn-out epic of its building was fraught with problems, excitements and quarrels worthy of a soap opera, and recognition must go to those who picked up the pieces after Utzon left and made the visionary designs into reality – Ove Arup and the engineers who calculated the structures, and the Sydney architects of Hall, Todd and Littlemore who succeeded in inserting a functional interior of concert hall, opera house, cinema, theatre and restaurants into the soaring while sails on a low podium which Utzon had dreamt up. Yet, what emerged from its long and arduous birth trauma is a most imaginative and expressive set of reinforced concrete shells sited on a spectacular mole jutting out into Sydney harbour, just beyond the shadow of the great bridge. It is a building worth going across the world to see.

CHAPTER ELEVEN

THE CONTROLLED ENVIRONMENT

As we have already seen, the fundamental characteristic of the architecture of the 20th century is its exploration of space. With that, comes the technological control of spatial conditions both within and without the designs. In the northern hemisphere, it is mostly within. The result should be – and often has been – better conditions for work and living. The materials are available, none more definitive than glass. The techniques are also known. It is worth devoting a brief chapter to the subject because it is often underrated as a factor in the history of modern buildings.

The essence of the problem is the creation of good conditions of lighting, heating and ventilation, and the necessity for the users of a building to be able to control them. The creation of good conditions has been notoriously variable in results; the availability of individual controls is the most important part of the present state of development.

In the years following the Second World War, the changes in lighting technology led to a gradual change in the way lighting is considered in relation to architecture. For most of the history of architecture, the development of lighting has been only the changing design of light fittings. The source of artificial light – whether it be flares, torches or candles – has hardly changed. Even with the invention of gas lighting in the early 19th century and that of electric lighting in the latter part of it, the essential use and treatment of light did not change fundamentally except that more and brighter light was available. It was stage lighting that took the initiative in using light for effect without seeing the source; and the arrival of film, and later television, significantly extended the possible effects gained by manipulating light. It took a little longer for architects generally to recognize what had happened in such special fields and extend it to the architecture of everyday housing and working.

One of the first changes – in the '30s – was the introduction of concealed lighting in houses and cinemas. It was often as uninteresting as the architecture it was intended to reveal and it

was only later developments that led to the design of lighting as either a permanent display or as a changeable, flexible system, giving the controller the ability to transform an interior by selective switching. One of the best examples, by a professional lighting designer, is that of the interior concourse spaces of the National Theatre in London, 1967–76. The lighting becomes an essential part of the spatial design, as significant as planes of colour in the cubist interiors of the International Style. That is logical, for the architect of the National Theatre, Denys Lasdun, was a major exponent of that style.

The ability to control heating and ventilation as well as lighting made possible the new landscaped interiors of the '60s and '70s. The pioneers of vast internal spaces – the atriums of big hotels and public buildings and offices – were in the United States. John Portman's Hyatt Regency Hotels became the paradigm of controlled internal environments. Versions and variations of them appeared in many parts of the world, notably in Hong Kong – soaring internal spaces, with sleek glass lifts rising at one end and planting dripping from every gallery, became almost standard. The theme spread to shopping centres and supermarkets, with ramps and glass lifts and trailing plants. The essential condition for them was a satisfactory controlled internal environment, with comfortable heating, cooling and ventilation. The introduction of computer-assisted controls, with feedback mechanisms so that adjustments could be automatic as conditions changed both outside and in, completed the necessary technology. There was now no reason, other than cost, why the interior environment should not be as calculated as the structure and as comfortable for living as the most delightful external environment.

That the results in general have been disappointing and have contributed to the degradation of the ordinary environment,

National Theatre, South Bank, London: Denys Lasdun (1967–76)

The National Theatre, by Sir Denys Lasdun, one of the descendants of Tecton, stands at the far end of the South Bank arts complex from the Festival Hall. Although not as gruesome as the Hayward Gallery, and despite meticulous attention to shuttering, its concrete exterior is unattractive. Its three theatres serve every kind of drama: the largest – the Olivier – has an open stage; the intermediate – the Lyttleton – a proscenium arch. The Cottesloe provides a shed-like little theatre for experimental and more intimate work before an audience of just 2–400, in accordance with the fashionable progressive ideas of an era which produced The Place in conjunction with the Royal Shakespeare Theatre at Stratford, and The Studio, attached to the large Crucible Theatre at Sheffield. Fly-towers express the two larger theatres on the exterior, and terraces cantilevered out on the river side add to exterior interest and social facilities. However, it is the interior spaces, partly achieved by setting the Olivier at 40° to the Lyttleton and by lighting technology, that are the triumphs of the building.

represented by hundreds of standard, repetitive office blocks and slabs of housing, is a measure of the lack of expertise and experience among architects and builders, and more especially, of the cost. The controlled environment cannot be cheap. Its successful manifestations have therefore been among public and commercial buildings in places where energy was available.

In the United States, the prolific firm of Skidmore, Owings and Merrill, which had acquired an international reputation through the Lever Building in New York, produced some of the first wholly-conditioned landscaped interiors. Such interiors were, in fact, an importation from Germany where the landscaped office – or Bürolandschaft – had been introduced. In Britain, Foster Associates and Building Design Partnership created some of the most satisfying landscaped offices – open offices whose work stations are carefully spaced and planted to create an environment suitable for working. Foster's offices for the insurance brokers Willis Faber and Dumas at Ipswich have impeccable conditions as well as a unity of interior space assured by the constantly moving escalators at the heart of the open-planned building. The most celebrated feature of the building is, however, the envelope of mirror glass wrapped round the exterior, which reflects the constantly moving people and vehicles and clouds. The life of the building both inside and out becomes part of its design.

It was a relatively small step from the design of a controlled environment to what has come to be known as 'High-Tech' – that is, the combination of high style and technology. In Britain, its apostles were Norman Foster and Richard Rogers. That it emerged more dramatically in Britain than in countries with better or more advanced technology was due to an extraordinary English episode in the 1960s. Seeking for a way to exploit technology in much

Peachtree Plaza Hotel, Atlanta, Georgia and Hyatt Regency Hotel, San Francisco: John Portman

With his Hyatt Regency hotels which, as architect, Portman has designed and as a developer, built, a new era of structural virtuosity combined with an exotic environment has opened for rich hotel-dwellers across the world. Such hotels can now be found from America (where they started) to Australia, with Hong Kong and other ports of call in between.

Outside they may well be clothed in smooth glass or concrete slabs; inside is a fairy cavern with such luxuriance of glass, foliage, balconies, canopies, spiral walkways, bridges and sculpture as to imitate a particularly luxurious Baroque garden. Characteristically, the centre of the building is an open landscaped atrium, surrounded by galleries dripping plants with transparent capsule-lifts zipping up and down, while at different levels cocktail waiters thread their way between tinkling fountains or round tinkling grand pianos that float on pads projecting into lily ponds.

(Opposite page, above)

Halifax Building Society, Halifax, Yorkshire: Building Design Partnership (1974)

The building rises like a great liner above the terraces of Halifax. A controlled environment makes life pleasant for the workers, and the retrieval system of title-deeds is like a high-tech skyscraper city in itself.

Willis Faber & Dumas Building, Princes Street, Ipswich: Norman Foster Associates (1975)

Doubts about the urban use of reflective glass are dispelled by this heart-shaped building bounded by a total wall of glass. Foster Associates brought the building right to the edge of the irregular site, and the glass from sky right down to the ground where it is boldly slotted into the pavement of a busy street without any protective devices to mar the line. The continuous glass wall is made of a series of strip-facets, each of six panels, hung from the roof-frame; the panels are bolted together with almost invisible metal corners. In the words of Kenneth Frampton, the glass proffers 'a range of constantly changing kinaesthetic sensations, opaque and scintillating in overcast light, reflective in sun, transparent at night.' It is one of the world's most sophisticated instances of glass technology. The circulation corridor running round the edge of the building while the work goes on at desks in the gloomier interior has been criticized, but this is offset by some highly mechanized environmental control of the working conditions. Features include central circulation spaces with plants and escalators, a swimming-pool on the ground floor and a restaurant and terrace on top. The roof is grass, and the green carpet of the restaurant appears to drift outside where a man may sometimes be seen mowing the roof.

broader terms than just the structure of buildings, a group of teachers and students in the Architectural Association School in London, calling themselves Archigram, published the first edition of their magazine, also called *Archigram*, in 1961. Its editor Peter Cook said that its inspiration came from the space comic; 'its reality is in the gesture, design and natural styling of hardware new to our decade – the capsule, the rocket, the bathyscope, the Zidpark, the handy-pak.'

With brilliant graphics and a readiness to attack all conventions and try every image, Archigram produced a stunning variety of Utopian projects. The most famous were *Plug-in City*, in which prefabricated metal boxes containing flats, shops and offices could plug in to a gigantic grid of tubes containing all the services; and the *Walking City*, an horrific image of a city with even more gigantic legs and the same plugged-in components. There was

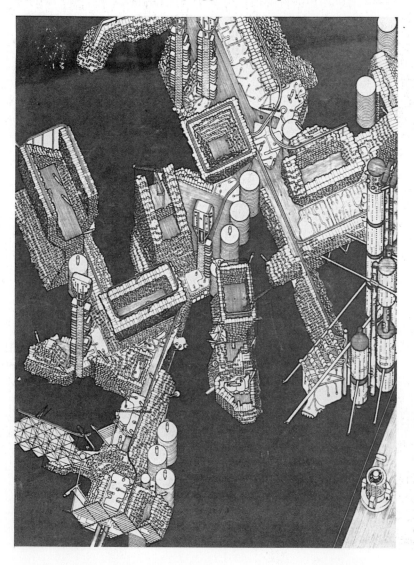

Plug-in City: Peter Cook and Archigram (1964)

This vision of the disposable city of the future, designed to last 40 years with the minimum elements replaceable at three-yearly intervals, was the brain-child of the Archigram Group at the Architectural Association School in London – Peter Cook, Warren Chalk, Ron Herron, Dennis Crompton, David Greene and Michael Webb. The city was a machine made of a grid of tubes to house the service infrastructure that is usually below ground; box-like buildings would then be clipped on to the grid when and where required. This is space-age, Superman-architecture of architectural happenings, guided missiles and electronics. Critics should respond with 'Wow!' and 'Bam!'

never any evidence of a demand for such megalomaniac structures other than the fantastic imaginations of the authors. But their influence was world-wide; a symbol, and eventually the reality, was the overhead crane which could pick up prefabricated boxes and rearrange the city's components if the inhabitants so desired. In Japan, the Metabolist school of design advocated expendable and changeable city blocks. Kisho Kurokawa's Nakagin Capsule Tower was the first – and possibly the last – direct application of Archigram's principles.

It was Norman Foster's Hong Kong-Shanghai Bank, finished in 1986 and reputedly the most expensive commercial building ever erected, that became the symbol of High-Tech and the expression of advanced technology. Its structure was original, with great frames from which suspension structures support groups of floors in 'villages' in the air; its components, for example the modules for

Nakagin Capsule, Tower Hotel, Tokyo: Kisho Kurokawa (1970–2)

Japan's developments in industrialized systems of prefabrication are among the most advanced in the world. Kurokawa took up the Archigram theme for the hotel by providing a framework for a plug-in system of small living units comprising a bath, double bed, kitchen, storage and sitting area, all in a space measuring eight by twelve feet. Each unit has its own controls for heating, ventilating and air conditioning. To the observer, it is rather like an ancient Japanese wood puzzle or the interlocking geometry of their timber temple structures. Kurokawa's own explanation of the interlocking box-like units with central port-hole window is that 'they're bird cages. You see, in Japan we build concrete-box birds' nests with round holes and place them in trees. I've built these birds' nests for itinerant businessmen who visit Tokyo, for bachelors who fly in with their birds!'

(Left)

Yamanashi Press and Radio Centre, Kofu, Japan: Kenzo Tange (1964)

The clipped-together impermanence of the Metabolist school contrasts sharply with the permanence of the snow-capped Mount Fuji range below which this building is set. The structure is totally expressive: the office and studio ranges form bridges between cylindrical towers in which the services are housed. The beams do not always run regularly from side to side of a façade: they break off halfway to give a sensation that others can be slotted in or taken away as the need arises.

Hong Kong – Shanghai Bank, Hong Kong: Norman Foster (1979–86)

The layered skyscraper of the Hong Kong-Shanghai Bank adds to the already extraordinary skyline of the Hong Kong waterfront that greets visitors coming in on the ferry from Kowloon – yet another aggressive finger thrusting skywards from the rock. But a skyscraper with a difference: it is the most advanced piece of technology of our day. Aware that in most skyscrapers all the drama is on the exterior, while the internal office-space, like the requirements of bureaucracy, is often repetitively filled in in triplicate, Foster sought new ways of varying internal space. The basic tower is made up of three slabs of 28, 35 and 41 storeys, and these are again broken down into areas with which workers can identify by having lifts stop only at selective floors, dividing the towers into units of four to seven floors. These are the 'villages', and each has its social area of restaurants and recreation spaces, two floors in height, between it and the next 'village'. Spatial experiences are also given by the moving staircases which carry most of the traffic of the building. These sweep up from an enormous atrium at ground level, lit by 'an array of computer controlled mirrors that move (with the sun) during the day'. 'The difficulties of building rapidly and quietly on a tight site have been resolved by a combination of technologies', says Foster. He chose the best technology for each job, from manual power to high-tech. 'The fastest way to place caissons is to hand dig them', he notes, adding that this is also noise free; and the scaffolding used for building was the usual webs of bamboo common to every building site in Hong Kong. At the other end of the scale he used the Concorde design team and, fittingly for an architecture of spaces, the technology of the Space Programme. Sadly, many of those who have been inside it find it glossy and cold – too perfect to be pleasurable.

Handwritten annotation on image: • Lloyd's Building • Beaubourg

Centre National d'Art et de Culture Georges Pompidou (popularly known as Beaubourg), Place de G. Pompidou, Paris: Piano and Rogers (1971–7)

service rooms, were imported from other countries; its assembly methods were original and effective; its composition, notably at the top, with the crane required by Archigram and a helipad, suggests an open-ended approach to design far removed from formal perfection, an architecture of visible change and expendability.

The influence of Archigram was present with even greater force in the most celebrated and popular of all modern buildings – the Pompidou Centre in the Place Beaubourg in Paris, designed by Richard Rogers and Renzo Piano, 1971–7. In order to create floors of uninterrupted space inside, to house a gallery, a library, and an electronic workshop, all theoretically flexible and adaptable for other uses, Rogers turned the building – in effect – inside out. The escalators run in transparent tubes up one side of the building and the service pipes, which would normally be in ducts inside, are as the other side, grouped in rows and finished in bright primary colours. The result is to make the exterior a scene of fun and action and colour, like a huge mechanical fairground; and a fairground it has become, with acrobats, fire-eaters, buskers and tumblers entertaining the crowds who come to see the outside of the building, not the inside – an exact reversal of one of the basic tenets of the Modern Movement.

In his next major building, for Lloyd's in the City of London, Rogers effectively played the same game by forming corner towers with shining steel components and thus displaying stairs, lifts and

The rear façade of this building, covered in coloured pipes and ducts, along a section of dusty Paris street in not-the-best quarter, looks at first like the back of an industrial plant to the visitor who looks for something impressive in the fashion of classical Paris. The other side, where the open *place* slopes down to the building, is where the action is – everything from pizzas and flower-sellers to snake charmers and escapologists, while overhead colourful people slide diagonally up the face of the building in transparent plastic elevators.

A massive building, Beaubourg has the classic reversals of contemporary architecture – it is inside out, upside down and back to front. It was completed on time and on budget, but a certain amount of the flexibility that was the point of

putting all the services on the exterior was lost by cost-demands forcing the mezzanines, intendedly moveable, to become fixed. The engineering consultant and designer of the structure of steel tubes and joints with tension cables was Peter Rice of Ove Arup & Partners. Inside, it is really not very interesting and ramshackle lifts make it difficult to get access to all floors for those who do not want to use the elevators; but many problems must be due to its popularity: it is used by five times as many people as was estimated in the brief.

Lloyd's Building, 107 Leadenhall Street, London: Richard Rogers (1981–6)

It is suitable that the ancient London institution of Lloyd's insurance exchange should be sited in the heart of the City. The building itself owes nothing to tradition. A concrete building, like Beaubourg, Lloyd's is 'inside out'. The service core running down the centre of the traditional office tower has been removed and replaced by an atrium that is glass-roofed, and runs up the full height of the building – the 'market-place' where the work of the exchange takes place. Offices are grouped round this open core, and services are relegated to six 'satellite towers' adhering to the outside of the building. The technology of the services is therefore easily accessible for maintenance and replacement. The very virtuosity of this building makes people hope it will be unique. Arthur Drexler speaks with horror of the prospect of a Paris full of Beaubourgs. A Lloydsified London, all grey pipes with a black straightened-out Thames as proposed by Rogers at a recent exhibition in the Royal Academy, fills one with equal horror.

pipes on the outside, leaving the internal floors free for dealing. The services work well and both buildings can be regarded as examples of High-Tech. What is less clear, is whether the services are real or decorative. Unless all the pipes on the Pompidou Centre are functional, it can only be the appearance, rather than the reality, of advanced technology that is a dominant factor in design. These two chapters – on the dynamics of spatial structures and the controlled environment – contain some of the most powerful arguments for and against modern architecture. On the positive side, there can be no doubt of the popular successes in the design of spatial structures. Not surprisingly, the most spectacular are structures for sports, dance and exhibition halls which are social centres attracting large numbers of people and demand great spaces which encourage adventure and experiment. There can also be no doubt of the vast improvements in the servicing of buildings, in the development of controls that can be manipulated by hand or computerized.

On the negative side, it must be questioned not whether exterior pipes and lifts are beautiful but whether they say anything about the nature of modern architecture. Is their use fundamentally different from the use of any other decorative feature put there for no other reason than to make the exterior more interesting?

The same question must be asked about the expression of the structure, as well as the services, of a modern building. Mies van der Rohe's tall blocks for offices or apartments give an impression of simplicity, emphasized by the rolled steel joists on the exterior, which are not in fact structural but decorative – applied to give an impression of structural honesty rather than reveal the reality. Foster's Hong Kong-Shanghai Bank poses the same problem. What appear as structural members in the great frame are in actuality the metal sheathing which hides the fireproofing materials surrounding the real structural members hidden within. The simple expression of structure has been made further impossible in every country by fire protection. Has the theory supporting such designs been made obsolete?

Throughout the history of architecture structural economy and honesty have rarely, if ever, been the *real* inspiration. Rather it has been the appearance that matters. For example, the triglyphs and metopes on the friezes of Greek Doric temples are decorative features derived from the timber construction of earlier temples. They were rejected by modern architects because of their irrelevance, but it is difficult to see why they should not be just as relevant or irrelevant as the decoration of a building whose structure is hidden behind fireproof materials. Neither tells the literal truth. The justification for the expression of structure and services rather than historical detail is that it is an expression of the age – the age of technology, the inspiration for a style.

CHAPTER TWELVE

CONSERVATION AND RENEWAL

Vernacular Architecture

The Conservation movement, which must be recognized as a significant element in the formation of the architecture of our time, originated formally in England. It did not confine itself to that country though for long. By the second half of the 20th century, it had become an international movement. The Society for the Protection of Ancient Buildings was founded at the suggestion of William Morris in 1877 as a corrective to the huge scale changes being made by the Industrial Revolution and the transformation of towns and cities as more and more old buildings were demolished or badly restored.

Not surprisingly, it was a similar surge of massive rebuilding in the years following the Second World War that stimulated the movement to keep old buildings and improve them. In Britain, it was focused by the foundation of the Civic Trust in 1957 and by the legislation and changes of policy that followed the Civic Amenities Act of 1967. But it was not only a British phenomenon. In France, Germany and Italy it was just as effective; and in the United States the movement took shape in the 1960s with Government legislation concerned with preservation. Until that time, the movement had depended upon individual initiatives in different states. The most celebrated exercises in the renewal of city centres were those of Philadephia started in the 1960s and on a smaller scale, the restoration of Annapolis and colonial Williamsburg. In Eastern Europe, the movement concentrated more on massive and impeccable restoration – in some cases total rebuilding – of historic buildings after the War.

The destruction caused by the War was only one factor and it did not affect every country. Instead most rebuilding was due to the great building boom of the late '50s, '60s and '70s – an economic phenomenon accompanying the rise in population and changes in industry. In the midst of massive expansion, some outstanding new buildings were erected; but the public and professional dismay being increasingly expressed concentrated on two main areas of development – city centre office building and mass housing. The movement that aimed to correct the worst excesses of poor development was Conservation, whose purpose in Great Britain was not simply to preserve old buildings but to preserve *and* enhance them (and indeed whole areas) for the benefit of the community. Like the Modern Movement in its earlier stages, the Conservation Movement had a social dimension.

The symbol representing the end of the Modern Movement and the arrival of the Conservation Movement is sometimes awarded to the demolition of the Pruitt Igoe flats in St Louis in 1972. They had been designed by a leading architect, Yamasaki, and received awards from the American Institute of Architects. Nevertheless, they had become disfigured by arson, vandalism, graffiti and excrement. A few years later, similar demolitions began in Britain.

At the same time, in continental countries and the United States, rebuilding and restoration became more popular. The Corbusian vision of large buildings in space was found as unsatisfying as ever. It now seemed that the old city blocks were what people liked and wanted, the muddle of the traditional city was life and vigour. What had advertised itself as a democratic social architecture was now seen as a totalitarian Utopianism, which however much it might satisfy its designer and promoters, was profoundly disliked by the ordinary observer and user of the buildings.

So, on the one hand traditional styles had a revival, sometimes literally, sometimes wittily when recreated in new materials and with strange juxtapositions. But, more fundamental than that, the idea of Conservation became an important element in architecture. What one writer described as the 'past, present and future in continuum' was now seen as a creative element in design. The movement set out to redress the general public's belief that in any development, the new buildings would be worse than the old buildings whose place they were to take – what could be more satisfying and a happy compromise than to keep as much of the past as possible and use it as a guideline for the design of the new? Such items could transform an area and make it into a new unity, with the best of the past and with any luck the best of the present – all brought together in a conserved landscape.

That was primarily the concern of town planning. In most European countries and in America and Australia, significant areas of towns were designated conservation areas – areas in which buildings, both great and small, and their surroundings would be given special consideration with a view to preserving the best of the buildings, and enhancing the whole area. Typical of

such areas were the precincts in the centre of great cities which became foot streets, where vehicles were excluded either for the whole or part of the day. In Britain, this followed the Civic Amenities Act and the subsequent town planning Acts.

The way in which the Conservation Movement affected individual new buildings had three main variations. The first was what came to be known as the Neo-Vernacular Movement or Style. As we saw in Chapter Three, an interest in traditional vernacular architecture has been a constituent element in the search for a new, free architecture since the end of the 19th century. Now, after the rejection of the vernacular by the International Style – for anything vernacular was by definition local or regional and not international – and in reaction against the anonymous rectilinear architecture of flat roofs and square corners, architects began to look again at the ordinary buildings of the past. Such buildings mostly dated from before the Industrial Revolution, but they also dated from the period when the vernacular had again been popular – the turn of the century.

One aspect of those influences was the revival of Edwardian architecture, sometimes unconsciously but mostly consciously in Britain where terraced and semi-detached housing and even large new buildings such as shopping centres and hotels were constructed in the Edwardian manner. It frequently manifested itself in the revival of traditional, sometimes rustic features known to be more functional than, for example, flat roofs – steeply pitched roofs, small windows, string courses on exterior walls, dormer windows to reduce the height of the upper floor. Most of these were not the

City Hall, Bensberg, Germany: Gottfried Bohm (1965–7)

Using concrete (which at that stage was still thought to be the most economically viable material) Bohm built his City Hall into the ruins of a circular mediaeval fortress with such success that its courtyard has become the central gathering place in the town.

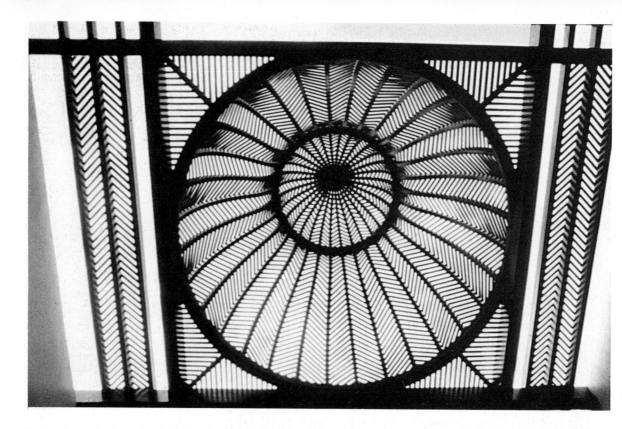

fruit of a style, but the details of a functional tradition. Vernacular architecture, being not consciously styled but the result of a pragmatic solution to repeated problems, must be more relevant to an architecture that rejected historic styles.

The Neo-Vernacular therefore has many faces. In the Middle East, after the oil boom, there was a conscious search for identity; any regional architecture had been destroyed and the new buildings were at first similar to the complexes familiar in the West. In doing so, it seemed to architects after the first building boom that they were taking from the West a style of architecture which was probably the worst in its history. The search for a new regional architecture took many different forms. In Jeddah, for example, the new Suleiman palace was unmistakably modern but inspired by traditional materials and by the factors which the architect considered a key to design – the sun, the desert and the spirit of the people. It was a search for roots, for the continuity of the past and present and future.

The new buildings for the University of Qatar of 1985 were similarly inspired by the vernacular architecture that had been developed to deal with the climate, catching the wind and funnelling it through small courtyards like small oases. In Kuwait, the water towers were striped, mushroom forms. The airport was more modern, a conscious image of a bird, by the Japanese architect Kenzo Tange. With the Parliament building, Jørn Utzon, the architect of the Sydney Opera House, created a great

Wooden Lantern above Courtyard, Suleiman Palace, Jeddah: Waled el Waku (1986)

The precipitate growth that followed the oil boom put the architecture of the Arab States into a spin, but the climate and traditional Islamic patterns are reasserting themselves and this part of the world is now producing its own form of modern on a strongly traditional basis.

University Buildings, Qatar: Kamal El-Kafrawi (1985)

Qatar gained independence from Britain in 1971 and soon became aware of the need to educate its students at home. The university, by an Egyptian architect, now houses 15,000 students. The site is a desert hillside 15 km N of the capital, Doha. The architect worked on an octagonal module which answered the need for small, well-equipped

Water Towers, Kuwait: Lindstrom

The mushroom-shaped water-towers bring together two of the essential elements in traditional middle eastern architecture: water and shade. There is also more than an echo of the ubiquitous palm tree.

lecture-rooms; these may be smaller or taller according to need, and are grouped into a variety of honeycomb arrangements. The units normally grow into towers, some box-topped, some slatted, some capsule-shaped with round wide lattice-covered windows. These have technological functions: the 'sunlight towers' diffuse light into the library; the wind-towers act like chimneys in reverse, stretching up into areas of wind-movement above the desert heat and sucking in fresh air. The architect tried to make use of natural, non-expensive elements. The walls are precast in a two-layer sandwich, with outer modulor panels and special insulating materials on the inside. The entire complex can be crossed without encountering violent changes of temperature.

National Assembly Building, Kuwait: Jørn Utzon (1986)

Utzon aimed for an architecture of simplicity and clarity based on the Arab countries' new awareness of their natural heritage. All elements are prefabricated concrete in dazzling white; much lies open to an intensely blue sky. The large open lobby faces the Persian Gulf. Sagging swags of concrete form roofs over the walkways, between columns scooped out in longitudinal ovals to create fern-fingered supports. Utzon combined the elements by his 'additive' method, which he feels produces extendable natural groupings 'with the same effect as the addition of trees in the forest or a Danish lunch, depending on how many different elements are introduced to the game. ... In this way it can grow like a tree; if it grows naturally, the architecture will look after itself.'

concrete canopy using the image of a Bedouin tent and achieving something of the dignified stillness for which the tent had been known.

In Britain, the most celebrated public exercise in the Neo-Vernacular was the Civic Centre at Hillingdon in Greater London. It is a deceptive building because the inside is an open office plan, with wide spaces and uninterrupted views, whereas the exterior is a complex series of pitched roofs of differing heights and widths, with a mass of valleys, ridges and gutters. The brick exterior uses moulded bricks with corbel tables and sloping plinths – a vernacular, if not very English, building on the outside and a modern international building on the inside. A more consistent and integrated use of the vernacular, using a more rural, Cotswold character, is the conference centre at Minster Lovell by Edward Cullinan. Also, on the edge of the river in the city of Durham, the shopping centre at Millburngate by Building Design Partnership seems a natural and unpretentious part of the urban fabric.

The second manifestation of the Conservation Movement was the revival of some historic styles. This was something entirely contrary to the original ideas of the Modern Movement, which saw the rejection of historical styles – and indeed style as such – as fundamental to a new social architecture. The announcement of the end of the Modern Movement was made by Charles Jencks, American architect and critic resident in Britain, who coined the phrase Post-modernism. He identified the taste of the first phase of the Post-Modernist era as Post-Modern Classicism; and indeed in both America and Britain it was classical taste that was revived most dramatically. Within a short time, Gothic was revived – for skyscrapers.

(Opposite, above)

Hillingdon Civic Centre Offices, Uxbridge, London: Robert Matthew Johnson Marshall (1971–6)

Andrew Derbyshire was the partner responsible for these government offices which house the social services for the area. Although the internal offices follow a more orthodox pattern, the red brick and single roofs, the pattern-work of small units joined together with a jumble of little roofs like a mediaeval village, was designed with the express purpose of creating a non-bureaucratic, homely and approachable environment to welcome the public. A crucial factor in the planning was the decision to depart from the normal roof inclination and vary the angles, so that some roofs are much steeper than others.

Centre for Advanced Study in the Developmental Sciences, Minster Lovell, Oxfordshire: Edward Cullinan with Julian M. Bicknell and Julian Wickham (1969–71)

Cullinan is a master of the rehabilitation of older buildings (popularly known as 'rehab') as can be seen from his church at Barnes. Here, three existing buildings were incorporated into a study centre of Cotswold vernacular character. The former L-shaped house supplied a reception area, dining, service and office areas. An old malthouse that had been used as a garage was transformed into a library block; and a T-shaped barn provided conference rooms. A new block of bedrooms was placed between the house and the conference rooms. The college atmosphere was extended with a flagged cloister and, opposite it, a bridge crossing the river topped with grass. The same architect's designs for a visitors' centre at Fountains Abbey promises equally to combine functional and technical requirements with a building utterly at home in its environment.

In the revival of styles, there were two identifiable approaches. One – more popular in America than in Britain – was the use of a style as caricature, an exercise in architectural wit. To that category belongs Charles Moore's Piazza d'Italia in New Orleans, with Ionic volutes in stainless steel and brightly coloured columns – a jolly pastiche of short-lived value. More serious because bigger, but still an exercise in wit, was Philip Johnson's A T & T block in New York, with a skyline said to resemble a Chippendale piece of furniture with a broken pediment. The block succeeds in recapturing some of the excitement of the pre-war New York skyline that was lost when the International Style left the city with flat topped towers, none more blatantly uninteresting than the huge twin towers of the World Trade Centre.

Of the more serious copyists of historical styles, the most successful were Leon Krier, working in both Germany and Britain, and in Britain alone, Quinlan Terry and Robert Adam.

Far more significant and influential in affecting the taste for styles, was the finding of new uses for old buildings. Different in principle from the restoration of historic styles because that was

Millburngate Shopping Centre, Durham: Building Design Partnership (1972–6)

This is an area of strong architectural interest in a historic city. The shopping centre borders the river and merges unobtrusively into the attractive townscape with buildings of many eras that step up the hill. In the best traditions of a true conservation area it looks across to the castle rock and the Norman Cathedral which is one of the wonders of Europe, and is close to Ove Arup's very beautiful and very contemporary bridge.

Piazza d'Italia, New Orleans: Charles Moore (1979)

For Urban Innovations Group, Moore erected a sort of stage-set, or Mannerist joke, full of classical quotations in the Italian quarter of the city – columns, arches, colonnades, cut off and with the orders all wrong, capitals, some in highly polished aluminium, water running through an arch, a pool shaped like the map of Italy – even neon lights. All it needs is some of Paul Michel Jarre's electronic music, some fireworks and a play of lasers. When this sort of crazy collection of architectural bits was assembled at Portmeirion, Wales by Clough Williams Ellis, it was considered endearing eccentricity; now it is Post-modernism.

essentially a creative activity, such architecture required an attitude of mind and a vision of inherent possibilities to which the architect trained in the ethos of the Modern Movement seems peculiarly suited. And it involved both historical knowledge and contemporary vision, especially the vision of space which is fundamental to the modern mind. The essence of the problem is to see the possibilities in an old disused building and change and repair it, restore its most valuable features and then create a new concept in which the surviving parts are integrated in a new unity.

The finding of new uses of buildings and complexes and then successfully adapting them was an international phenomenon, in direct contrast to the assumption that the new environment would require wholesale demolition. Of the redesign of complexes of buildings, the most famous was the conversion of Pier 17 in South Street, Seaport, New York, into a leisure centre with shops, cafés and play areas. In London, after protracted public controversy, the market buildings at Covent Garden Market became a new shopping centre with specialized shops and – again – a social centre with cafés, restaurants and outdoor performers.

The re-use of old buildings has included many building types and many new uses, some of them surprising. Churches in London, Edinburgh and Oxford have been converted into concert

American Telephone & Telegraph Building, Madison Avenue, New York: Johnson/Burgee: Simmons (1978)

Inside, the A T & T Building is orthodox skyscraper office accommodation. The exterior is peculiarly arresting, the broken pediment on the top contriving to catch the eye above, round or in between other skyscrapers wherever one is in the chasms of the Manhatten streets. The interest probably lies in a design for something small-scale, like the back of a Chippendale chair, executed in not merely large but (as can be seen from the entrance arch) giant proportions.

Battersea Power Station, Nine Elms Lane, London: Giles Gilbert Scott (1929–35, 1944–55)

The architect of Liverpool Anglican Cathedral and the designer of the classic red British telephone box was the author of this landmark of industrial London on the Thames. It once heated the housing schemes of Battersea with its waste-product, but now, like the telephone boxes, it is declared redundant. In the days when the mammoth turbine house was clanking and pulsing wih life, it was said to resemble the forges of the giants of mythology. However, the exterior with its chimneys on the four corners, in spite of Scott altering the engineers' 'pedestrian elevations', has been said to bear the more domestic appearance of a kitchen table turned upside down.

Pier 17, South Street, Seaport, New York: Benjamin Thompson & Assocs (1985)

Mayor Edward Koch opened the last link in the project for the regeneration of the 19th-century waterfront in Lower Manhatten. The 100 foot high shed of steel and glass, the metal-work painted vivid red, projects out into the river. The architects wanted a 'muscular and everyday character' situated on a seafaring site. It has been converted into a pleasure area by day and night with a delight of seafood restaurants, glassed-in arcades, boutiques and seaside shops, open-air cafés and bars. The open-air decks command distant views of the opposite waterfront and Brooklyn Bridge.

Covent Garden Development, London

Since the vegetable market moved, the area has been developed as a social centre. A market area with hand-crafted goods is interspersed with rows of small shops. Cafés abound: groups of white tables allow patrons to watch the live entertainment which goes on all the time. Further development, including extensions to the Opera House by Jeremy Dixon and BDP, is in the design process.

All Saints Church, High Street, Oxford: Robert Potter of Brandt Potter Hare Partnership (1975)

This 17th-century collegiate church of nearby Lincoln College was declared redundant in 1972. To convert this oblong box composed of three by five 15 foot bays into a library, changes made in the 19th century had to be rectified and the floor raised in one area. Wood from a disused altar piece in Magdalen College was re-used.

halls, the storage of archives and libraries. In France, a monastery has become a youth centre; in Italy, a convent has become a university faculty; in Montreal, a convent has been converted into offices, shops and a restaurant. Barracks in Portsmouth, England, have become a museum – the simplest new use for an old building. More adventurous was the turning of an 18th-century Gothic temple at Stowe into a holiday house and a carriage house in New York into a theatre. In Massachusetts, some farm buildings have become a school art centre; in Norway, an archaeological museum. An obvious conversion into a museum was that of the Moorside Mills at Bradford in Yorkshire; wholly successful and internationally famous was the use of the Old Maltings at Snape in Suffolk as a concert hall and arts centre.

An arsenic mine in Cornwall has become a holiday home, some ice houses at San Francisco, California, wholesale showrooms, and a railway station at Brunswick in the German Federal Republic has become a bank. Perhaps the most adventurous – and successful – was the total conversion in London of the Markenfield Road pumping station and sewage works into a children's playground.

In Scotland, the most popular of all new buildings in the last decade has been the Burrell Collection Building by Barry Gasson in Glasgow. Burrell had made a huge collection of all sorts of works of art and design, including parts of ancient buildings. In creating a wholly new gallery in a park, Gasson used the forest trees on one side behind a glass wall as a feature; elsewhere, he incorporated old features like a huge doorway, bits of old panelling and stained glass. That was an original exercise in conservation, in which new and old form what has often been intended – the continuity of the past and the future in a building that is unmistakably of the present.

Probably the best of all projects in bringing new and old together was the housing scheme at Byker in Newcastle (1969–80). Its architect was Ralph Erskine, an Englishman who moved to Sweden in 1939 and admired the fact that its architecture was regional rather than international. The Byker development was one of the most complete exercises in public participation, in which the future residents were able to express their opinion about the shape and character of the buildings they wished to see. The site being beside a new motorway, Erskine protected it from noise by creating a long serpentine wall of housing whose bricks are of different colours forming a dramatic abstract pattern. Within the space created by the wall are smaller terrace houses with gardens. There are shed roofs, informal fences and original entrance structures, the whole environment adding up to a colourful, thickly planted, domestic scene. The continuity of the past and the future is unmistakable.

Burrell Collection, Pollock Park, Glasgow: Barry Gasson (1972–83)

Barry Gasson built some of the exhibits from the collection of antiquities, paintings and ceramics of an eccentric Scottish ship-owner into his spankingly modern museum. Entry through a Romanesque gateway from a 16th-century Yorkshire castle directs the visitor into a vast glass atrium in the centre of which plays a massive classical lead basin fountain from Chatsworth. Glass walls and roof not only saturate with light all the things one wants to dwell on – the exhibits, the greenery, the exposed and crafted joints and beams of the rafters – but also allow Pollock Park to drift in on a green tide.

Byker Re-development Housing, Newcastle-on-Tyne: Ralph Erskine's Arkitektkontor AB (1969–80)

Byker is interesting both as the first emphatic break in Corbusier-inspired, high-rise, post-war housing, and because it anticipated the vogue for the 'community architecture' of the '80s, promoted by sociologists like Alice Coleman and architects like Rod Hackney. The commission was to build re-housing for 9,500 residents displaced by the removal of Victorian terraces to make way for a projected motorway. The 'Byker Wall' of undulating housing (sometimes eight storeys high, sometimes three or five as it follows the contours of the site) was built along the site perimeter to back on to the motorway (which was never built). Behind is a village of little houses built of different materials, with balconies, lean-to sheds, communal landscaping, footpaths, bright colours, many flowers and bushes, washing hanging out and old men sitting on seats – all combining to give the lie to the often proved fact that communities can never be planned overnight but must be allowed to grow organically across centuries. This was achieved by first building a pilot scheme of 46 dwellings in nearby Janet Square, and using them to provide feedback into an architect's surgery set up in a former undertaker's shop in the site.

There appears to be no end to the possible uses of well built, old buildings. And what is significant in the context of this study is that most of them are not prestige buildings but industrial, vernacular buildings. The vernacular has become the inspiration for architecture again.

CHAPTER THIRTEEN

AN ARCHITECTURE OF PLURALISM

The demise of the International Style described in Chapter Eight was probably less significant than the continuance of an intellectual habit fundamental to it – the belief that each problem should be thought out afresh. That meant that any assumption about modern architecture should always be challenged, every programme for a building considered *de novo*. A lot of time would be wasted as young architects set about painfully solving problems that had been solved satisfactorily many times before. But the process succeeded in eliminating a lot of outworn conventions and it ended any authority of the historic styles. Architecture could never be quite the same again.

The immediate result was to reject the use of any styles that had reigned in the 19th century, or been modified and vulgarized in the 20th. It soon became clear, however, that it was difficult to design in no style, to reject all the styles and discover a valid architecture relevant to everyone because it was not to the taste of any one particular group. The International Style was, after all, a style like any other and not the inevitable result of meeting social and technical demands without preconceptions. Its rejection, in turn, opened the architectural portfolio to any style that might be in the offing.

In the absence of a consensus, architects began to design in a bewildering variety of ways, inventing styles of a personal and ephemeral kind, more confusing and less convincing than anything invented in the 19th century. In case the differences were not obvious in the buildings themselves, an elaborate vocabulary of styles was invented, confusing the scene more than the architecture could – concepts like Personalism, the New Rationalism, High-Tech Corporatism, Expressionism, Post-Modern Classicism, Responsive Anarchism, Romantic Pragmatism and Structural Dynamism could be multiplied endlessly. More straightforward were such comprehensive categories as the vernacular and community architecture, easier to announce than to define.

The implication was that the search for authority in architecture had to be reinvented. But it had now to be an authority more basic than before. If the conventional styles would not suffice and the architecture was to be relevant to the age, the authority must be fundamental. An attempt had been made to base an architecture upon basic materials, *objets trouvé*, materials as found or made, notably raw concrete. Defined as Brutalism, it failed for it was too unattractive to please anyone but the architects who used it. But it represented the same need that had been expressed by architects at the turn of the century – the search for reality – and it provoked again the same question that has been asked throughout the history of the art; what is the reality of architecture? The person who knows that answer can design with conviction.

Finding the answer is probably more difficult today than at most earlier periods of history for two reasons. First, while the actual programme of building may vary in each country from decade to decade, on a world scale it is colossal, and we know more about it through the media than ever before. While one place is celebrating a major development, another is upsetting the *status quo* with a new style.

Second, the scope of choice is wider. It is possible to try anything for technology has transformed the possibilities. In architecture, too, the development of systems of structure and the servicing of buildings has widened the parameters of design. Anything can be considered; and that removes the very limitations that used to discipline the development of a style. In the light of technology transformations, there are theoretically no limits to the height and width and depth and bulk of buildings. The scale can be bigger, more unrelated to anything, than ever before.

The materials available are also more varied. Most are traditional, but plastics, used more in components than for total structures, have introduced a new lightness and flexibility into design. Of the older materials, the most definitive changes have been made in glass – now as transparent and translucent as before but also produced in larger, flatter sheets, coloured, reflective, glare resistant, variable in its transmission of light and heat. The overall shapes of buildings have revealed unprecedented possibilities. Conventional junctions may disappear and with them traditional details. Walls and windows can be treated as one continuous membrane; walls and roof may be treated as one; the three-dimensional composition can be massive or irregular or crystalline; the colour more positive or transient. The possibility of a polychromatic urban landscape is real and exciting.

The obvious result is an architecture of pluralism. First, the building types designed by architects are different and more varied. Housing, the commonest of all building types, was not in the past the business of architects; since the turn of the century it

Guild House, Philadelphia: Robert Venturi and Rauch (1960–3)

The street façade steps back in three sections from either side of a dominant entry panel on whose wide central window opening, striped with balconies and headed with a round-topped segmental window, attention is focused. This Friends Housing for the Elderly was intended for local people. Venturi hoped to give them the environment they were accustomed to, tapping 'congenial associations' and a 'commonly held imagery'. So, he built a block of flats on the street line, of cheap bricks and with the standardized windows used in the cheapest housing schemes nearby (from which the occupants may well have come). The final patronizing touch is the anodyzed gold television aerial which surmounts the flat roof-line – 'a symbol of the aged, who spend so much time looking at TV'. One looks at the dismal six-storey block in a dusty, litter-scattered street, and remembers how it was Le Corbusier's social principles that engendered the Unités.

House in Chestnut Hill, Philadelphia: Robert Venturi and Rauch (1962–4)

Venturi built for his mother a variation on a suburban bungalow by splitting the gable in two to reveal (down the crack) another block rising behind it. This is a deliberate good-bye to the pure glass box of International Modern and a return to the homely gable, the sloping roof, the porch, the dormer: all is forgiven. Venturi said of it: 'This building recognizes complexities and contradictions: it is both complex and simple, open and closed, big and little; some of its elements are good on one level and bad on another; its order accommodates the generic elements of the house in general, and

Chair: Venturi

The nursery-rhyme quality in Venturi's invention crops up again in this spotted, or herbaceous, chair fit for Pooh to sit on.

has been, often on a giant scale. Country houses have become fewer, but expensive private houses, like those designed by Gaudi or Le Corbusier or Lloyd Wright, have been seminal buildings for the Modern Movement. Cathedrals and churches less so, but they have provided opportunities for special display and structural innovation. Factories and railway stations, which were monuments of 19th-century urban expansion, continue to be built, especially in the third world. But for the most part the characteristic building types for modern architecture are schools, colleges and universities, concert halls, museums and art galleries, sports centres and stadia, hotels and restaurants, airports, power stations, shopping centres and supermarkets.

Second, the types of solution are as various as the types of building. For example, the prolific American architectural firm of Skidmore, Owings and Merrill has itself produced an architecture of pluralism. The firm has produced a seminal international building with Lever House, New York and then a giant demonstration of structural dynamics with the Hancock Tower in Chicago. It has also been symbolically expressive with the Airforce Academy at Denver, Colorado, romantically historicist with the airport terminal in Jeddah and, as if to disprove any assumptions, has given an occasional display of the vernacular.

Other architects vary their serious or solemn designs with exercises of wit and originality. Of the witty productions, one of the best was Casson's Elephant House in London Zoo, as bulky as its inhabitants and as heavily shaped. London Zoo was already the home of architectural experiments like Lubetkin's Penguin Pool, now it had a veritable cathedral for elephants. In America, Robert Stern found an appropriately witty form for the Best Stores in which a whole section of wall rolls away as if falling down and reveals a sophisticated shop behind.

Exercises in historic styles, perhaps because it is difficult to design in those styles while keeping the face straight, tend nowadays to be just as whimsical and superficial as the obvious witticisms. Michael Graves' celebrated Public Services Building in Portland, Oregon is Aztec in style on the outside, but an ordinary office block inside. Philip Johnson's even more celebrated A T & T building in New York is elegantly styled outside and finished at the top with its so-called Chippendale broken pediment; but it is also an orthodox office block inside. Much more serious in concept, if equally bizarre in effect, is the work of Leon and Robert Krier, apostles of Rationalism, whose projects for Berlin reflect a desire to restore form and order to it and recreate a pre-Industrial European City, with an order lacking in the post-Corbusian modern city.

Inevitably, as in other periods of history, some architects have gone to extremes. Modern technology having extended the possibilities for experiment in both structural design and the servicing of buildings, some weird fabrications have appeared – underground houses, dwellings shaped like arteries or intestines, bones and crustaceans as well as capsules. Never more than oddities, they nevertheless illustrate the same fundamental characteristic of all modern architecture – its understanding of the manipulation of space.

Another 'solution' in the search for reality can be found amidst the euphoria in the creation of unprecedented spaces. Some of the

Elephant House, London Zoo, Regents Park, London: Casson and Conder (1964)

The new elephant and rhinoceros pavilion was built as part of the Zoo's redevelopment plan of 1956, and won an RIBA award in 1966. The beautiful bulky forms in reinforced concrete, scored to show the aggregate, resemble its slow ponderous inhabitants. Curved walls faced with grey-blue tile inside make for easy cleaning.

Public Services Building, Portland, Oregon: Michael Graves (1980–2)

Considered by some to be insensitive to its site, this is a white and black punctured cube. Graves has criticized architects like Mies van der Rohe for failing to make entries explicit; here a vast area of dark-tinted glass 'window' (some of it covering areas of concrete walling) volubly indicates the entrance. It has massive exterior detail in Aztec style and an ordinary office interior.

most dramatic and Expressionist have been in Germany. Gottfried Böhm, the son of a famous church architect, worked at first mainly on churches, of which the Pilgrimage church at Neviges, 1965–8, is a striking concrete crystalline composition. It is no less sculptural inside. His town hall at Bensberg again uses mass concrete, piling up and sharply sculpted to form a fantastic three-dimensional climax.

The most celebrated exponent of such Expressionist architecture was Hans Scharoun (1893–1972). After the Second World War, Scharoun became Director of Housing in Berlin and was involved in its replanning. What crowned his long career and established itself as one of the great modern buildings of Europe was the Philharmonic Hall in Berlin, 1956–63. Relatively plain and awkward outside, inside it is a fascinating exercise in spatial planning with varying levels of seating like trays suspended in space around a central platform. It is space seen in movement or completed by the movement of people within it, probably the most complete Expressionist masterpiece of its time.

The fourth aspect of the present scene is displayed in cities in most parts of the world and is the contrast between the giant commercial buildings and the human scale of buildings for day-to-day living. High buildings continue to be used for housing, probably more successfully when expensive for at least the lifts work then. Most high buildings are commercial – sometimes, as in New York, Hong Kong and Tokyo, concentrated in ever decreasing spaces; sometimes, as in Paris, prohibited in the centre and concentrated on the outskirts; more often, as in Britain and Germany, springing up in different parts of the city.

The skyscrapers, which were one of the formative components of the architecture of the turn of the century, have grown bigger and higher in the last 30 years. They have to be seen as vast geometrical statements, of a scale never known before and now capable of shapes and colours unknown in the early skyscraper years. They may be semi-disguised with patches of colour, as in the huge tubular housing blocks at Nanterre in France; but more often, in many parts of America, the glass cladding is reflective and coloured, resulting in a glittering brown or golden or green urban landscape.

In New York the latest skyscrapers have recaptured the variation of skyline of the older skyscrapers, like the Chrysler Building. In other cases, they are planned as tight groups of towering forms like the Bonaventure Building in Los Angeles or the Sears Tower in Chicago. But the biggest concentration of giant architecture is in Texas, especially in the work of Johnson, I. M. Pei and Welton Beckett, in Houston and Dallas.

While buildings get bigger and bigger in some areas, where money is in abundant supply, in others a more humane, smaller

Pilgrimage Church, Neviges, Germany: Gottfreid Böhm (1965–8)

It appears that an iceberg has been deposited in the little town, heaving its jagged bulk up to tower over the roofs. Inside, the play of facets of moulded concrete in the vault are equally awesome.

Philharmonic Concert Hall, Berlin: Hans Scharoun (1959–63)

The pet name for this building – 'Karajan's circus', so-called from its conductor and tent-like interior – testifies to how it has caught the popular imagination. The orchestra occupies the central space in the auditorium surrounded by 2,200 seats in irregularly shaped tiers. Together with the folds of the concrete roof, these replace the mouldings and statues of Victorian concert halls, giving a superb acoustic. The interflow of spaces and vistas from foyers at different levels and the cascading grand staircase make a case for expressionism.

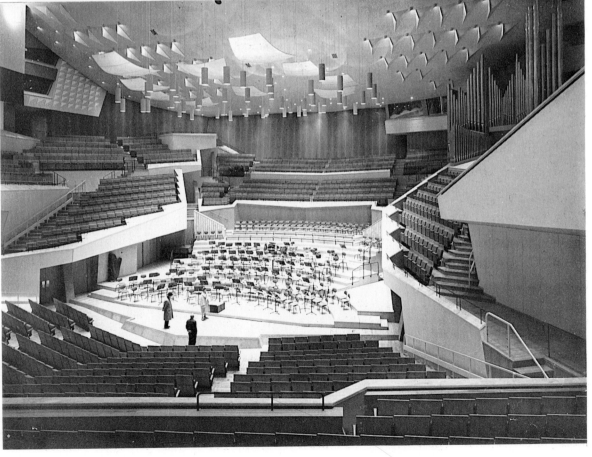

(Far left)

Chrysler Building, New York: William van Alen (1928–30)

For a few years before the Empire State skyscraper was built, the Chrysler was the world's tallest building. In three sections, it is stepped inwards while retaining its rocketing upwards surge. Still in the period when New York's tall buildings broke out on top into a skyborne town of churches and palaces and monuments, the Chrysler breaks out into '30s cinema architecture with an extraordinary spire, scalloped with interlacing arches. After Chrysler came the bland point and slab blocks of International Modern.

Torre Velasca, Milan, Italy: Belgiojoso Peresutti and Rogers (1957–60)

A brief that called for both office and apartment accommodation encouraged a courageous break with the faceless skyscraper tradition. This original building has sympathies with the mediaeval fortress towers in the locality. The stem of the 26-storey tower holds offices. The top eight floors of living flats spread out on enormous concrete brackets four floors deep. The fenestration looks as if somebody has thrown a handful of windows at the façade.

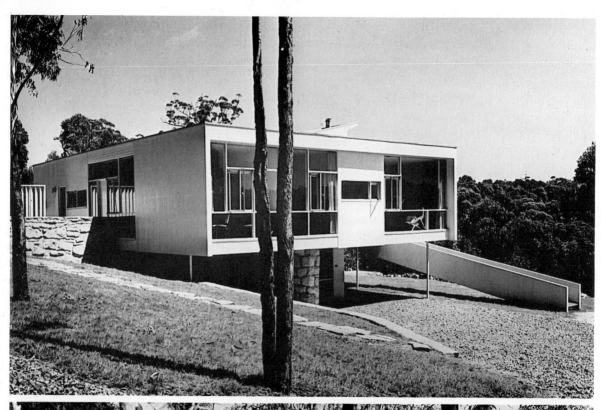

scale, architecture has been emerging, making much of the landscape and achieving a dignity through careful control and clarity of detail. In Australia, houses by Harry Seidler and Peter Johnson are good examples. In Britain, some of the best new buildings were the product of the sudden expansion of the universities and colleges in the '60s and '70s. Of these, outstanding are the work of Powell and Moya, such as the Cripps building at St John's College, Cambridge and Arup Associates work at St John's College, Oxford. In Switzerland, the group of architects known as Atelier 5 applied Le Corbusier's ideas for mass housing to a steeply sloping site and created a series of terraces more varied and informal than any of the monumental projects of Le Corbusier himself.

The extreme variety, confusion and chaos of this contemporary scene, this expression of pluralism and personalism, may be more apparent to architects and architectural critics than it is to the average observer and user of the buildings. To them, much modern architecture seems all the same, unexciting, bleak and repetitive – as, indeed, much modern architecture is. Only occasionally does a special building take the breath away. But when it does so, the results are as exciting as anything in history. Utzon's Sydney Opera House is a popular success. So is Rogers and Piano's Pompidou Centre, Meier's Museum in Atlanta, Gasson's Burrell Collection building in Glasgow and Stirling's Staatsgalerie in Stuttgart.

We must therefore ask what they have in common, if indeed, they do have anything in common. First, they are all social buildings, for people anxious for contact and community, for the excitement of happy accidental meetings and unusual experience. As such, they achieve the very opposite of the isolation of individuals in huge blocks of housing and they illustrate that what brings people together in architecture is not repetitive units grouped closely together for day to day existence but something unusual, special, memorable – a shared experience of excitement that can be recollected in tranquillity. Second, such buildings have the excitement of the very characteristic special about modern architecture – the excitement of space – Le Corbusier's *l'espace indicible*: the miracle of inexpressible space.

In the development of such an enriched and intellectually resonant modern architecture, the most effective figure was Louis Kahn (1901–74). An immigrant to America from Estonia but trained in America in the Beaux Arts tradition, Kahn was at first a follower of the International Style and a member of CIAM's Team X. In the early '50s he travelled in Greece and Egypt and that seems to have revived his love of historic architecture, seen now not as an item for study but as a field of knowledge capable of analysis, interpretation and use in creating a new form.

Seidler House, suburbs of Sydney, Australia: Harry Seidler (1948–50)

Seidler was a pupil of Breuer and worked under Niemeyer in Rio de Janeiro. He brought the ethos of American domestic contemporary architecture with him to Australia in 1947 and achieved a new national character in the house he built for Rose Seidler. 'The pioneering days of modern architecture are over. We are now in a period of consolidation and development,' he has said. The sloping site was cut away and a white box inserted, balanced on a platform of rough rubble foundations. A gangway leads up to the door.

Johnson House, Chatsworth, Sydney: Peter Johnson (1963)

Rough clinker bricks and slatted wooden balconies have prompted allegations of a 'brutalist ideology' behind the house Peter Johnson, Professor of Architecture at Sydney University, built for himself just outside Sydney. In fact, it grows out of the ground – not just any ground but out of this boulder-strewn, sloping piece of virgin Australian bush. There are no formal gardens: far from the bush being tamed, it is entered into. Natural flowers, shrubs and trees sprout luxuriantly right up to the door; parakeets and Australian bush babies scuttle around the balconies eating nuts put out for them.

(Opposite, above)

Cripps Building, St John's College, Cambridge: Powell and Moya (1967)

The Cripps building supplied rooms for undergraduates and fellows as part of the great expansion of the universities in Britain in the '60s. The building staggers its way between other buildings. Finish is high on materials which include unclad white concrete, polished concrete, Portland stone, bronze window frames and lead facings.

Sir Thomas White Building, St John's College, Oxford: Arup Associates (1976)

Hostels in the Oxford college were grouped in an L-shape to form another quadrangle with existing buildings. The interest is in the scale, in the relationship of pavilion blocks of different heights to the parent buildings. As in the Cripps Building there is meticulous detailing.

Goetheanum II, Dornach, near Basel, Switzerland: Rudolf Steiner (1928)

Goetheanum I, built as a 'free high school of spiritual science' was destroyed by fire on New Year's Eve, 1922–3. Goetheanum II was its replacement built to Steiner's designs. In reinforced concrete, in a plastic moulded form as full of shelving cubist planes as a Braque landscape it has an outline quite as original and eccentric as the mind of its author (who had founded the quasi-religion of anthroposophy). Various colleagues and disciples completed the main and surrounding expressionist buildings after his death, including the strange boiler-house with its plantlike, Gaudiesque chimney.

'I believe,' he said, 'that the architect's first act is to take the programme that comes to him and change it. Not to satisfy it but to put it into the realm of architecture, which is to put it into the realm of spaces.' It was a significant change of emphasis. It meant that the programme, which had been the starting point for design in the orthodox Modern Movement, was not enough or could be a false start. The essential meaning of architecture would not be found from a functional diagram. Rather, it needed an imaginative leap to discover the reality, to establish that the building was profoundly what it was meant to be – that is, the very *type* for the programme. That underlying meaning was the essence of the problem and the key to architectural form.

Kahn's output was not huge but it was hugely influential. A turning point was the Richards Medical Research building in the University of Pennsylvania in Philadelphia (1957–62). It was a seminal building at a critical moment of change. He made one of those intuitive leaps of thought that he considered essential to the formulation of the idea for a building. Analysis of the building's requirements revealed that as a research laboratory it would need large flues for ventilation as well as substantial ducts for mechanical services, stairs and lifts. The crucial element in his act of creation was his recognition that it was the spaces for services and communications that could be fixed and the spaces for laboratories that needed to be flexible. It was a moment of simple revelation that was to affect architectural thinking for years to come. He formulated the idea of *served* and *servant* spaces and used the distinction as a key to the plan. The service towers on the edge of the building were the fixed and dominating elements, a perimeter of open-ended towers that earned the laboratories the nickname of *Ducthenge*. The laboratories and other study rooms could be flexible within that overall structure. Kahn probably got the idea from his study of Frank Lloyd Wright's Larkin building; the expression of services rather than public spaces was to influence buildings in many parts of the world in the next few years.

In that building, and even more effectively in later ones, Kahn used the primary geometrical forms – the square, the circle and the triangle – and grouped them together in plans to make a complex composition or used them as features in the fenestration. In the dormitories for the college at Bryn Mawr in Philadelphia, in the massive developments in Dacca and Ahmedabad and most expressively in the Kimbell Art Museum at Fort Worth (1966–72), he created memorable social spaces; the museum became a social meeting point for people at leisure. He combined his feeling for history with an understanding of solid geometry and fused them through his unusual vision to create some of the most monumental architecture of the 20th century. Of that, the most original

Siedlung Halen, Berne, Switzerland: Atelier 5 Group (1960)

Adventurous, pigeon-hole ranges of post-Corbusier housing, the Siedlung Halen lies along hill terraces and has the powerful presence one associates with Lowland Mayan palaces.

Museum, Atlanta, Georgia: Richard Meier

By Corbusier out of Classicism, Richard Meier's work is concerned with cutting up enclosures of space both vertically and horizontally. The sequence of external and internal spaces he created for this museum and auditorium, has, as at Stuttgart, produced an environment so popular that it has become a Sunday meeting place.

Richards Medical Laboratories, University of Pennsylvania, Philadelphia: Louis Kahn (1957–62)

The outline suggests an Italian defensive towered town like San Gimigniano. Bordering one of the main routes through the campus, and with much-turreted, neo-Gothic baronial older buildings nearby, Kahn designed the laboratories as clusters of tall, narrow towers. The opposite to the kind of building where all the elements are wrapped together under one skin, all his elements are separate, the joints and connections purposely on show. He took a new look at function by deciding that since scientific research constantly changes, the permanent parts of this building were the service areas housing important necessities like the vast extractor flues. And so

these units are the smooth, brick shafts which catch the eye; the columns of glass-boxed laboratories on a concrete frame are attached in a cellular fashion. Kahn may have considered architecture the 'thoughtful making of spaces' but spaces here have not proved very satisfactory. Entry spaces are mean, and connecting corridors become clogged with trolleys, people and equipment, impeding circulation and blocking functional flexibility. Lack of protection from sun and glare in the glass laboratories gives another ground for criticism.

National Assembly Buildings, Sher-e-Banglanagar, Dacca, Bangladesh (formerly East Pakistan): Louis Kahn (1963)

Kahn set his Parliament Building at the fulcrum of his complex; the smaller buildings, such as the hostels, radiate away in staggered groupings in a V-shape. Their forms are those of square boxes or drums, and they zig-zag along the waterside like crinkle-crankle walls. Into these forms (with no frames to detract from the geometric purity) are sliced door and window openings in the shape of triangles or the segments of a circle. The Assembly Building itself is a mandala of superimposed geometric forms: within an octangular plan, circulation space, press and members' rooms girdle the central chamber. These patterns of shapes and spaces direct the search for the 'spirit' of the building which Kahn felt lies beyond function. Here, says Drexler, he 'came closer than ever before to an architecture that transcends time and place.'

Kimbell Art Museum, Fort Worth, Texas: Louis I Kahn (1966–72)

Cool, classical, in meticulous good taste, the galleries have diffused lighting from glassed-in ridges running down the centre of curved vaulted ceilings in concrete.

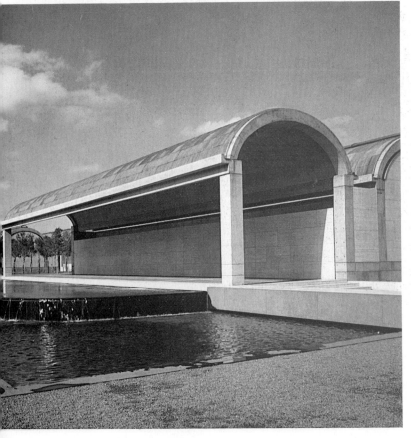

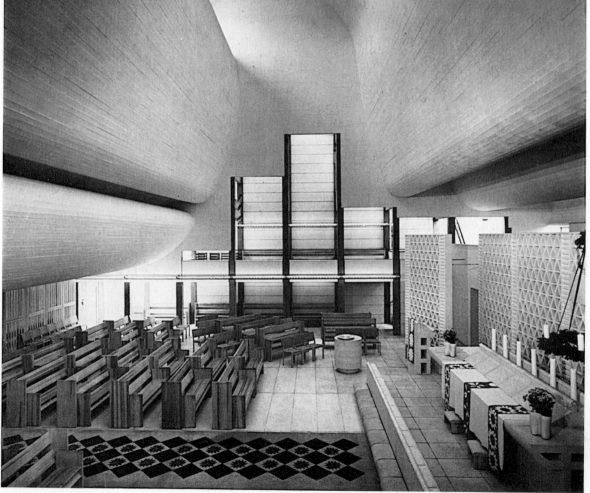

– and apparently inevitable – were the geometrically impeccable Government buildings at Dacca, Bangladesh.

If Kahn was responsible for the rediscovery of monumentality in public architecture, it was Jørn Utzon who provided the utmost excitement with his competition winning design for the Sydney Opera House. The difficulties in its erection, the resignation of the architect before its completion and the fact that the interior in no way reflects the soaring shape of the exterior cannot nevertheless detract from the beauty of the concept and its emotional impact at the end of Bennelong Point. Utzon does not belong to any one school of design. The Paliament building at Kuwait has a concrete canopy based upon a modern interpretation of the traditional Bedouin tent. In the church at Bagsvaerd near Copenhagen (1969–75), he incorporated a wave-like rising and curving ceiling for acoustical reasons which may resemble the ceiling he intended to place inside the Opera House, within an austere, rectlinear box-like exterior as undramatic as the Opera House is spectacular.

The architect who at the time of writing seems to bring most of the lessons of the modern architecture together is James Stirling. Recognized in most countries other than his own, he gained a national reputation in Britain in the '50s and '60s for housing and commercial work, but mainly for university buildings – at Leicester (with James Gowan, the Engineering Building, 1959–63), Cambridge (History Faculty Building, 1964–7), St Andrews (residential units for students, 1964–8) and Oxford (Florey Building for Queen's College, 1966–71). They belong to the mainstream of modern design in that their form is derived from a simple, if not naïve, expression of the main functional groups but distinguished by his apparently natural gift for the right proportion and scale. His later work, such as the new gallery at the Tate Gallery in London and his designs in other countries, is more formal and shaped by historical influences. Both his earlier and later work is, in an individual way, Expressionist – at first expressive of the hierarchy of functions, then expressive of historical antecedents. The Staatsgalerie at Stuttgart has warped shapes with glazing, stripes of different coloured stone, red and blue rails, ramps leading up to the gallery and through it; there are cheerful almost jokey details like the lift. It attracts the public in huge numbers, no less than 20,000 in a day, who may be going to see the building rather than the exhibits. The gallery thus functions in the same way as the museums in Atlanta and Forth Worth, as Sunday meeting places, for relaxation and fun.

Is it possible to summarize the present state of the art, seen through the work of many contemporary architects, especially through the work of the three architects isolated in this chapter? It would be rash to predict too exactly which work is likely to survive the ravages of historical changes of taste and enter the *corpus* of

Jonas Salk Institute for Biological Studies, La Jolla, California: Louis Kahn (1959–65)

Kahn looked to monastic patterns in designing for a group of scientists all intent with a quasi-religious fervour (as he saw it) on one area of research. The site was away from other buildings and looked out over the Pacific. Again, he separates out the functions of what Curtis calls 'the society of shared endeavour' from those of 'the private world of thought', into three clusters of buildings: the Meeting House, which comprised the meeting and conference areas; the Village of living quarters; and the parallel blocks of laboratories separated from each other by water gardens and connected by little bridges to individual study-cells.

Church at Taxvej, Bagsvaerd, Denmark: Jørn Utzon (1969–75)

On an unexceptional suburban site near Copenhagen, the church has an unexceptional exterior and simple plan for its complex of church, chapel and offices. But the whole internal space is covered in a licking white wave of concrete that in section appears to break and curl over in a great crest above the main space of the church.

Engineering Building, University of Leicester: James Stirling and James Gowan (1959–63)

The industrial red-brick and glazing of this controversial design has its roots in the 'frank' architecture of the Bauhaus. Most of the site is occupied by the long low block of the engineering workshops, distinctively top-lit through a continuous range of saw-toothed skylights, angled at 45 degrees to catch the north light. Attached to this is an irregular brick and glass tower of offices and tutorial rooms which grows up from a base of two, wedge-shaped, lecture theatres, cantilevered out and facing in different directions. There have been all sort of problems of noise, leaking, and glass glare on the computers (which of course were not there when the block was built); nevertheless, it remains assertive and impressive.

major architecture. What does, however, seem clear is that modern architecture, as widely interpreted as I have tried to do in this study, is by no means the arid scene of repetitive impersonality that has gained it the reputation of being boring. It is a period of great experiment, of challenge, of notable failures and even more notable successes.

There have been many flawed masterpieces and it may be that Le Corbusier's Pilgrimage Chapel at Ronchamp is the only universally recognized masterpiece of the 20th century. But in its time it too was a subject of much dispute; it took 20 years before it could be seen as the brilliant visionary work that it undoubtedly is. There is enough material being disputed today to give one confidence that ours will not be seen in history as a negative moment, but more likely as one of the great periods of innovation and experimentation in architectural history.

For it has done more than any period before to explore the potentials of structure, light and space and bring its discoveries together in a new, expressive unity. And more. Despite all the personal foibles and errant displays of arrogant self-expression, it has found its meaning finally among the social purposes for which it was first intended. But, as the Movement reaches maturity, it is no longer trying only to solve elementary problems of shelter for everyman; it has found real excitement and popular esteem in creating expressive spaces for community needs, where many people can share the raising of the spirit in a varied and provocative, but still civilized, environment.

Staatsgalerie, Konrad Adenaur Weg, Stuttgart: James Stirling (1984)

The design emerged out of three successive neo-classical designs for German museums and retains the dignified massing of classicism under an assembly of the light-hearted tricks of vivid colour and shape typical of Post-Modernism. The building is huge, encompassing, as well as exhibition galleries, a music academy, a workshop theatre and lecture theatre. But its size does not make it formidable. It is cut back into the hillside, bright colours and interesting shapes give a holiday atmosphere, and pathways cutting through the large central drum and onto different levels through a series of developing spaces make an architectural adventure trail.

CHAPTER FOURTEEN

THE NEW CONSENSUS

The enthusiasm for the conservation of buildings described in Chapter 12 – not only famous monuments but buildings of all periods and many types – was only partly a positive movement; it was also an expression of a general collapse of faith in the Modern Movement. The faith had been at its strongest when its results could not be seen but by the '60s, '70s and '80s, the evidence was only too clear. With more and more critical comments upon modern architecture in newspapers and on television, a great swing took place in public opinion. It seemed that people had awoken to the reality of what was happening to the environment around them – and did not like what they saw.

It was stated – and agreed – at innumerable meetings of the Conservation lobbies in America and Britain that it must be assumed that whatever took the place of existing buildings would be worse than what was there before. Such a lack of confidence in the creation of a new environment had happened before, notably in the 19th century; but never, it seemed, on the same scale. The public, as well as professional critics, were expressing a general dislike, if not hatred, for what architects had been creating for the last four decades.

Among the less articulate members of the public, the sign of this disillusion was a huge yawn – an expression of boredom with the new environment. It was a boredom created by the deliberate impersonality, the anonymity of the buildings of the International Style thought to be the essence of the Modern Movement. 'Architecture is not an art', said the painter Leger, 'it is a function of the social order.' As a celebrated artist of the period, he precisely described its dilemma. Mies van der Rohe put the position even more explicitly in a paper of 1924: 'We are concerned today with questions of a general nature. The individual is losing significance; his destiny is no longer what interests us. The decisive achievements in all fields are impersonal and their authors are for the most part unknown. They are part of the trend of our time towards anonymity.'

That the prophets of anonymity were frequently the most distinctive individuals themselves showed the inherent absurdity of the objective. But it nevertheless had a profound effect upon the architecture being produced. Almost anything interesting was being consciously eliminated. The search for an architecture so basic and common that no details would suggest the authority of the styles had to lead to bareness and simplicity, justified by the social imperatives of the movement. A reaction against it was inevitable. It was an architecture of social concern without personal understanding.

In the intellectual destruction of the theory of the Modern Movement, two books were profoundly influential. In America, Robert Venturi's *Complexity and Contradiction in Architecture*, 1966, shattered the image of general consensus. Aware of how bored people were by what he called 'orthodox modern architecture', he fastened the blame not upon the great pioneers like Aalto but upon the superficial, mindless architecture of the post-war years. A new richness of form and meaning would be uncovered by recognizing the essential ambiguity of good architecture with its 'several layers of meaning among elements with varying values'. So he was *against* the architecture of 'either-or' and *for* the architecture of 'both-and', of big and little, closed and open, continuous and articulated, of both good and awkward – in short, of complexity and contradiction.

He thus, to the delight and excitement of many young architects themselves worried by the emerging environment, rejected the orthodox sociological and technical definitions of architecture in favour of form and meaning, even if his own buildings were unexciting. In contrast to everything that had recently been said about towns and cities, he declared that 'Main Street is nearly all right' and attacked the system of town planning that had destroyed much of the city's vulgarity and life, expressed in flashing signs. He disliked the sculptural concrete boxes of the '60s and extolled the virtues of what he called the 'decorated shed'. His message was plain and immediate. He wanted a 'commonly understood imagery' – an imagery that the orthodox Modern Movement had conspicuously failed to discover. It might be found in the commercial strip and the despised suburban house, in the new vernacular.

In Britain, David Watkin's slim volume *Morality and Architecture* (1977), was an even more devastating critique of the thinking that had justified the Modern Movement. While recognizing and paying tribute to the scholarship of a great writer and teacher, he concentrated his critical analysis upon the work of Nikolaus Pevsner, which had illuminated 'a whole field on modern architectural history'. For it was Pevsner's *Pioneers of the Modern Movement from William Morris to Walter Gropius* (1936), that had established the ethos of the Modern Movement and identified the International Style as the apparently inevitable 'genuine and adequate style of our century.' It seemed inescapable. It 'fitted all those aspects which mattered, aspects of economics and sociology, of materials and function. It seemed folly to think that anyone would wish to abandon it.'

Watkin pointed out that it was essential to the argument of Pevsner's book that design, as a constituent of the as yet unrealized essence of modern society, was necessarily socialist. The Modern Movement was an expression of the *Zeitgeist*, or Spirit of the Age. In a devastatingly logical attack upon the very idea of the Spirit of the Age, Watkin pointed out the problem of the argument, which is its circularity. The Modern Movement is an expression of the Spirit of the Age; the Spirit of the Age is revealed by such phenomena as the Modern Movement in architecture. In Watkin's words, 'the supporters of this concern for total integration choose a certain kind of art and then fabricate a fictitious society which, in their view, is about to emerge and to which art must be integrated.'

The implications of his argument must now be taken further. For if architecture is the product of the political, social and economic conditions in which, and for which, it is generated, it must be more logical to look for variety and inconsistency in its manifestations, rather than the standard uniformity of the International Style. Society is clearly not standardized unless one holds the arrogant view that there is only one kind of society to which all countries and all peoples are inevitably bound to conform. But it was exactly this kind of Utopian totalitarianism which lay at the very heart of the theory of modern architecture. Its aim, as Mies van der Rohe insisted, was 'the suppression of the individual in favour of the collectivity'. Surrounded by the products of function and anonymity, society was now saying that it had seen enough of the collectivity; it would welcome some evidence of the individual.

In reaction against the standardized Utopianism of socialist theory, the fresh thinking of the '60s and '70s therefore called for a renewed emphasis on the individual rather than the repetitive formulae of standard building types. And it recognized the complexity of real design rather than the artificial simplicity achieved by following a narrow theory and ignoring the variety and confusion of individual tastes. The orthodox theory of modern architecture – or the theory of orthodox modern architecture – was at an end. What writers now looked for was a more humane theory, or what an author called a *modern* theory of architecture. It might even be that *any* theory of architecture would now be difficult to sustain.

Certainly no theory was found or announced that had any of

the certainty of Pevsner's. Architects continued to write bold
statements or war-cries or aphorisms, but none of them added up
to a coherent or systematic theory of architectural design. Perhaps
it was not a time for such a theory, for there was little or no
consensus about what is good or bad design, what is the
mainstream of modern architecture and what are aberrations
from it. In the absence of a central philosophy or social belief or the
authority of a recognized style, it might be described, as we have
just seen in Chapter Thirteen, as an architecture of pluralism.

On the other hand, at a time of protracted searching and soul-
searching, questioning and arguing, a time, moreover, when the
quantity of new architecture on a world scale was in no way
diminishing, it might be possible to identify some of the themes
that had been emerging and were recognizable in the architecture
of the 20th century. If so, it must be an architecture of much
diversity, not the single school of design now dismissed. The
problem with all art theory is that it tries to define art in terms of
everything except art; by eliminating all extraneous factors, it
attempts to reduce the concept to a simple statement as to what
art is. The same applies to architectural theory but could there at
least be an approach to modern architecture, which saw it as
architecture – not in sociological or political or economical terms –
just architecture?

If that is to happen, it must be a description of variety and
diversity, not of simplicity and certainty. To find out what modern
architecture is and can be, it must be false to narrow down the
search until only one possibility is left; it must surely be more
sensible to survey the scene in all its richness and diversity and ask
if any consensus is discernible, not in theory but in what has been
built. Such a pragmatic approach seems in any case more typical
of modern architecture, which is very pragmatic in its origins,
even if it is sometimes romantic in its results. Modern architecture
might be identified not be defining some meaning which is non-
architectural, but simply by describing and defining it as an
architectural *idea*. That is not simple or limited, for architecture is
one of the great synoptic activities in any culture, bringing
together the discoveries and perceptions of people in many other
fields and organizing them into some kind of recognizable unity.

In the search for a way of understanding modern architecture,
this book has attempted to explain the significance of each episode
or personality as one variation after another was added to a
wonderfully rich and varied tapestry of human endeavour.
Discoveries or perceptions have emerged throughout the century,
not just in one movement – or style – but usually overlapping with
several – and possibly ultimately with all. They include: the
fundamental study of the users' needs; the integrated design of
space both interior and exterior; an unprecedented control of the

physical environment; the recognition of growth and change as factors in design; the ability to achieve a new continuity, or flow, of spaces; the use of man-made materials, as well as the changed use of natural materials; a constant reference to Nature as a generator of form and structure; the persistent study of the vernacular as a clue to the architecture of Everyman; the renewed importance of the decorative arts; the possibility of unifying buildings and landscape; and the achievement of a consistency and totality at all scales for all artefacts.

The architectural methods for achieving such objectives are the same as they have always been – craftsmanship, proportion, the use of colour and the control of light. But certain factors play a larger part than they may have done in the architecture of earlier periods. In the control of the environment, both internal and external, for instance, there has been a greater emphasis on the calculation of natural and artificial light, of air conditioning and heating, especially of acoustics as a key element in devising new shapes for public buildings. Of all the materials available to the modern architect, the most significant in enabling him to control space and light and air is glass – not a new material but one transformed by modern technology – used not only for lighting and vision but for reflection and refraction, as a major walling material for enclosure and for structure. It is, of course, also an important material in electronics.

Bringing those themes together and subjecting them to examination in the light of the buildings isolated in this study, it seems to me that the following general themes are those that are characteristic of modern architecture:

1. Nature and growth as an inspirer of architectural form
2. The vernacular as a source of authority
3. Spatial understanding as the *sine-qua-non* of design
4. Solid geometry and mathematical proportion
5. Modern technology in the control of the environment
6. Continuity of form in the landscape of interior and exterior
7. A psychological unity of use, movement and experience

That list might suggest that we may have entered a new period of the Picturesque. At its peak in the 1790s, it was essentially a study in non-formal composition and the discovery of excitement in the fortuitous aspects often given by old buildings; it may be that the present concern with conservation is evidence of a new picturesque vision. In such a vision, the unity of any architectural composition must be accidental. It may even be that any attempt to achieve unity is less important than before; or it may be that there is a different kind of unity – a unity of use and experience, not of formal composition.

At the very least, a valid modern architecture cannot be one of anonymity and the simple expression of simple functions. But

whatever its individuality and diversity, there does seem to be one
central aspect which every designer insists upon and which, as we
have seen, is true of the technology of structure and of the new
environment, of interiors as well as exteriors. That is, the
obsession with three-dimensional space, as space made more
varied and unprecedented by the discoveries of modern physics
and engineering. And every articulate modern architect seems to
be aware of it. Even the apostle of anonymity, Mies van der Rohe,
said that 'Architecture is the will of the epoch translated into
space.' James Stirling explains that 'A design will start to emerge
in the imagination when the relationship of spaces appears to
have coherent organisational pattern.' Louis Kahn says in a
memorable sentence, 'Architecture is the thoughtful making of
meaningful space.' The importance and the extreme difficulty of
expressing this essentially architectural idea, so central to modern
design, has been best set out by Le Corbusier with his *l'espace
indicible'*.

   If the use, vision and exploitation of architectural space is the
ultimate distinguishing factor in modern architecture, it must be a
kind of space that is not quite the same as that of other periods in
which spatial design was most effective, such as the Baroque. It
has to do with continuity, made possible by structural and
physical discoveries – the flow of space which is mirrored by the
flow of people in movement, so that spaces are seen in movement
as well as moving one into another.

   Furthermore, there are three contemporary and important
aspects of architecture affecting our perceptions and enlarging
our expectations. The first is our increasing knowledge of world
architecture. With mass communications of many kinds, we are
better informed and have often seen a richness and variety of
which we can never have previously had first-hand experience.
The architectural lessons of the Middle and Far East, of Asia and
Central America, cannot be ignored – the remorseless logic of
western classicism has now to deal with a far wider vocabulary
than that which confronted Lutyens in India; we can even build it
on our own doorstep. They are lessons in colour and light and
form, in the relationships of inside and outside, in movement and
space, and the psychological power of unfamiliar shapes.

   The second is the accelerated pace of technological change. We
know more about the use of the temporary and the mobile, about
the organization of interior landscape and a controlled interior
environment; about the development and use of materials old and
new; about new uses for old materials – especially glass, now used
as a transparent medium, an insulating material, a structural aid,
a reflector. We know immeasurably more about the whole
apparatus of mechanical controls, especially electronic ones, the
use of process control equipment to compensate for heat, light and

humidity variations and to control the effects of sun and wind as well as heat and light, about microprocessors and computers that can give an instant diagnosis of faults and provide a better memory. The availability of systems that represent only a small fraction of the cost of a big building must mean that they will be increasingly employed. What that indicates is the possibility of being able to produce a controlled personal environment for all buildings. An architecture that exploits the new technology is capable of more variety, not less; it can be more complex, more colourful, more variable, more life enhancing.

The third important aspect of today's architecture is the new importance of landscape involving the total surroundings and the total environment of a building, as a crucial part of the concept of a design. The inside as well as the outside are involved and the resulting landscaped offices, landscaped houses and landscaped factories are an approach to design in which the landscape, and all the artefacts in it, are essential to the totality. The modern interior as well as the exterior is therefore concerned with change, with growth and movement and everyday care. And that involves a different kind of vision, more serial and three-dimensional, and an understanding of materials and the effect and use of light and heat upon them. It does not produce a static beauty but a changing one, perhaps a space which is never complete but part of a whole that is forever evolving.

Denys Lasdun, the architect of the National Theatre in London, has described this idea as follows, relating it to the life of a community: 'The concept of growth will be the generating factor in design and planning as were the rediscovery of Vitruvius' principles in the Renaissance. Some sort of flexibility will be built in as the key factor in tomorrow's architecture having as its task the making of a decent environment which will present people to one another and help them to a wider vision of life both as individuals and members of the community.'

It may be an architecture of apparent randomness that reveals, on enquiry, a deeply studied organic order, a non-immediate, but perceivable, unity of use and space. Its philosophy may be discovered in the collective endeavours of the community of design.

For the time being it seems that the complexity and contradiction of Venturi's book has been achieved, if not in exactly the way he meant. From the numerous variations, there appear to be two main developments in most parts of the world. They are what has come to be known as High-Tech (technological romanticism) and the Neo-Vernacular. But it may be that the lasting and real achievement of the Modern Movement was what the architects at the turn of the century wanted – to challenge authority and look anew at the task in the light of developments. In a paper delivered to the Royal Institute of British Architects in 1967, Sir Leslie Martin listed the 'three powerful lines of thought' that had characterized modern architecture in the '20s and '30s. They included the belief that there must be a complete and systematic re-examination of human needs, the full use of modern technology and the idea that each architectural problem should be constantly reassessed and thought out afresh.

If that is right, it must be a never-ending process. The challenge for architects is to fuse together technological advances with a renewed emphasis on the humane and the personal – on a human scale. Ultimately, architecture is an expression of human experience in the form of usable space.

INDEX

SELECTED BIBLIOGRAPHY

ALLSOP Bruce, *A Modern Theory of Architecture*, Routledge Kegan Paul, London, 1977
APPLEYARD Bryan, *Richard Rogers: a Biography*, Faber and Faber, London, 1986
ed. ARNELL Peter/BICKFORD Ted, *James Stirling: Buildings and Projects*, Architectural Press, London, 1985
ARTS COUNCIL, Catalogue for the Lutyens Exhibition, Hayward Gallery, London, 1987
ASLET Clive, *The Last Country Houses*, Yale University Press, New Haven & London, 1982
BANHAM Rayner, *Theory and Design in the First Machine Age*, Architectural Press, London, 1960
BENEVOLO Leonardo, *A History of Modern Architecture*, MIT Press, Cambridge Mass., 1971
BENTON Tim & Charlotte (eds) with SHARP Dennis, *Form and Function: a Source Book on the History of Architecture and Design 1890–1934*, OU Press, Milton Keynes, 1975
BILLCLIFFE Roger, *C. R. Mackintosh*, Academy Editions, London, 1977
BLAKE Peter, *Frank Lloyd Wright – Architecture & Space*, Penguin, Harmondsworth, 1960
CANTACUZINO Sherban, *New Uses for Old Buildings*, Architectural Press, London, 1975
CHASLIN, HERVET, LAVALOU, *Norman Foster*, Electa Moniteur, Paris, 1986
COLEMAN Alice, *Utopia on Trial*, Hilary Phipman, London, 1985
COLLINS Peter, *Changing Ideals in Modern Architecture*, London, 1965
CONDIT Carl W., *The Chicago School of Architecture*, University of Chicago Press, Chicago & London, 1964
CURTIS William J. R., *Modern Architecture since 1900*, Phaidon, Oxford, 1982
DAVEY Peter, *Arts and Crafts Architecture*, Architectural Press, London, 1980
DREXLER Arthur, *Transformations in Modern Architecture*, Secker & Warburg, London, 1979
ESHER Lionel, *A Broken Wave*, Penguin Books, London, 1981
FABER Colin, *Candela: the Shell Builder*, Architectural Press, London, 1963
FISHMAN Robert, *Urban Utopias in the 20th Century*, Basic Books, New York, 1977
FRAMPTON Kenneth, *Modern Architecture: a Critical History*, New York, 1980
FRANKLIN Jill, *The Gentleman's Country House*, Routledge Kegan Paul, London, 1981
GIEDION Sigfried, *Space, Time and Architecture*, Harvard University Press, Cambridge Mass., 1941
GIROUARD Mark, *Sweetness and Light*, Clarendon Press, Oxford, 1977
ed. GIRSBERGER, *Aalto* (2 vols), London, 1963, 1971
GRADIDGE Roderick, *Edwin Lutyens Architect Laureate*, George Allen & Unwin, London, 1981
GROPIUS Walter, *The New Architecture and the Bauhaus*, Faber & Faber, London, 1935
ed. HATJE Gerd, *Encyclopaedia of Modern Architecture*, Thames & Hudson, London, 1963
HITCHCOCK Henry Russel, *Architecture of the 19th & 20th Centuries*, Penguin, Harmondsworth, 1958
HITCHCOCK Henry Russel, *In the Nature of Materials: the Buildings of Frank Lloyd Wright*, New York, 1942
HITCHCOCK & JOHNSON Philip, *The International Style: Architecture since 1922*, Museum of Modern Art, New York, 1932
HOWARD Ebenezar, *Garden Cities of Tomorrow*, Faber & Faber, London, 1946
HUSSEY Christopher, *The Life of Sir Edwin Lutyens*, Country Life, London, 1953
IRVING Robert Grant, *Indian Summer*, Yale University Press, New Haven & London, 1981
JENCKS Charles, *The Language of Post-Modern Architecture*, Rizzoli, New York, 1973
JENKS Charles, *Modern Movements in Architecture*, Doubleday Anchor, London/New York, 1973
LAMBOURNE Lionel, *Utopian Craftsmen*, Astragal Books, London, 1980
LE CORBUSIER, ed. BOESIGER/GIRSBERGER, *Oeuvre Complête*, Thames & Hudson, London, 1967
LE CORBUSIER, *Towards a New Architecture*, John Rodker, London, 1927
LUTYENS Mary, *Edwin Lutyens*, John Murray, London, 1980
MacCARTHY Fiona, *The Simple Life*, Lund Humphries, London, 1981
MacLEOD Robert, *Charles Rennie Mackintosh – Architect and Artist*, Collins, London & Glasgow, 1983
MARTINELL Cesar, *Gaudi, His Life, His Theories, His Work*, Barcelona, 1975
MARTINELL Cesar, *L'arquitecte Gaudi*, Barcelona, 1976
MUTHESIUS Stefan, *The High Victorian Movement in Architecture 1850–1870*, Routledge & Kegan Paul, London, 1972
NAYLOR Gillian, *The Bauhaus*, Studio Vista, London, 1968
NAYLOR Gillian, *The Arts and Crafts Movement*, Studio Vista, London, 1971
NERVI Pier Luigi, *Structures*, McGraw-Hill, New York & London, 1956
NUTTGENS Patrick, *The Story of Architecture*, Phaidon, Oxford, 1983
ed. NUTTGENS Patrick, *Mackintosh and his Contemporaries*, John Murray, London, 1987
PEVSNER Nikolaus, *The Sources of Modern Architecture and Design*, Thames & Hudson, London, 1968
PEVSNER Nikolaus, *Pioneers of Modern Design*, Penguin, London, 1963
QUANTRILL Malcolm, *Alvar Aalto: a Critical Study*, Schocken, New York, 1983
RICHARDS J. M., *Guide to Finnish Architecture*, Hugh Evelyn, London, 1966
ROBINSON John Martin, *The Latest Country Houses*, The Bodley Head, London, 1984
SCULLY Vincent, *Frank Lloyd Wright*, New York, 1960
SERVICE Alastair, *Edwardian Architecture and its Origins*, Architectural Press, London, 1975
SHARP Dennis, *Modern Architecture and Expressionism*, Longmans, London, 1966
de SOLA-MORALES Ignasi, *Gaudi*, Academy Editions, London, 1987
STIRLING James, *Architects' Approach to Architecture*, Zodiac 16, Milan, 1966
SULLIVAN Louis H., *The Autobiography of an Idea*, Dover Publications, New York, 1956
TAFURI Manfredo and DALCO Francesco, *Modern Architecture*, Abrams, New York, 1979
TAYLOR Nicholas, *The Village in the City*, Temple Smith, London, 1973
VAN RENSSELAER Maruana Griswold, *Henry Hobson Richardson and his Works*, Dover Publications, New York, 1969
VENTURI Robert, *Complexity and Contradiction in Architecture*, Architectural Press, London, 1977
WATKINS David, *Morality and Architecture*, Clarendon Press, Oxford, 1977
WRIGHT Frank Lloyd, *A Testament*, London, 1957